Copyright © 2023

All rights

The characters and events portrayed in this book are fictitious. Any similarity to real persons, living or dead, is coincidental and not intended by the author.

No part of this book may be reproduced, or stored in a retrieval system, or transmitted in any form or by any means, electronic, mechanical, photocopying, recording, or otherwise, without express written permission of the publisher.

ISBN- 9798391765257

PREFACE

Preface

Dear Reader

Welcome to this fascinating exploration of quantum theory, the multiverse, and the impact of these ideas on our understanding of the universe and human civilization. This book is a comprehensive and accessible guide, designed to provide an in-depth introduction to the complex and often counterintuitive world of quantum mechanics, as well as its many applications across a wide range of scientific disciplines.

Throughout the course of this book, we will delve into the history of quantum mechanics, tracing its development from its inception in the early 20th century to the cutting-edge research and discoveries of today. We will examine the fundamental principles of quantum theory, such as wave-particle duality, quantum entanglement, and the uncertainty principle, and explore how these concepts have shaped our understanding of the nature of reality.

The book also investigates the fascinating topic of the multiverse, examining various theories and interpretations that propose the existence of multiple, parallel universes. We will explore how these ideas challenge our traditional notions of space, time, and the nature of existence itself.

In addition to the theoretical aspects of quantum mechanics, this book will also cover the practical applications of these principles, examining their impact on areas such as computing, cryptography, nanotechnology, and even biology and medicine. We will also explore the role of quantum mechanics in popular culture, including its influence on science fiction, movies, and television.

Furthermore, we will consider the ethical, social, and environmental implications of quantum technologies, discussing the challenges and opportunities that lie ahead as we continue to push the boundaries of our understanding of the quantum world.

This book is the result of a passion for both the elegance and the enigma that quantum mechanics presents. It is my hope that, by the end of this journey, you will have gained a deeper appreciation for the beauty and intricacy of the quantum realm, as well as an understanding of its profound impact on our understanding of the universe and human civilization.

Thank you for embarking on this exciting adventure with me. I hope you enjoy the journey as much as I have enjoyed writing it.

Sincerely,

J H W Williams

CONTENTS

Copyright
Preface
Quantum Realities: Unraveling the Mysteries of the Universe and Multiverse — 1
Part I: Foundations of Quantum Theory — 2
Chapter 1: The Birth of Quantum Mechanics — 3
Chapter 2: Key Concepts and Pioneers — 8
Chapter 3: Wave-Particle Duality — 12
Chapter 4: Quantum Entanglement and Nonlocality — 17
Chapter 5: The Uncertainty Principle and the Observer Effect — 21
Part II: Quantum Mechanics and the Universe — 25
Chapter 6: Quantum Fields and Elementary Particles — 26
Chapter 7: Quantum Cosmology and the Big Bang — 30
Chapter 8: Dark Matter and Dark Energy — 34
Chapter 9: The Multiverse and Parallel Universes — 38
Chapter 10: Black Holes and Quantum Information Paradox — 42
Part III: The Multiverse — 46
Chapter 11: Introduction to the Multiverse Concept — 47
Chapter 12: Many Worlds Interpretation of Quantum — 51

Mechanics

Chapter 13: Bubble Universes and Eternal Inflation — 55

Chapter 14: The Anthropic Principle and Fine-tuning — 59

Chapter 15: Brane Worlds and Extra Dimensions — 63

Part IV: Quantum Mechanics and Consciousness — 67

Chapter 16: The Quantum Mind Hypothesis — 68

Chapter 17: Decoherence and the Measurement Problem — 72

Chapter 18: Free Will and Quantum Determinism — 76

Chapter 19: Quantum Biology and the Origins of Life — 80

Chapter 20: The Role of Consciousness in the Universe — 85

Part V: The Impact of Quantum Theory on Human Civilization — 90

Chapter 21: Quantum Computing: The Next Frontier — 91

Chapter 22: Nanotechnology and Quantum Materials — 95

Chapter 23: Quantum Communication and Cryptography — 99

Chapter 24: The Role of Quantum Mechanics in Artificial Intelligence — 104

Chapter 25: The Future of Energy Production: Quantum Fusion — 108

Part VI: Quantum Experiments and Discoveries — 112

Chapter 26: The Double-Slit Experiment — 113

Chapter 27: The EPR Paradox and Bell's Theorem — 117

Chapter 28: Quantum Teleportation and its Applications — 120

Chapter 29: Quantum Superposition and Schrödinger's Cat — 124

Chapter 30: Recent Advances in Quantum Experiments — 128

Part VII: Philosophical Implications of Quantum Mechanics — 132

Chapter 31: Determinism and Indeterminism	133
Chapter 32: The Nature of Reality and the Role of the Observer	138
Chapter 33: The Problem of Causality in Quantum Mechanics	141
Chapter 34: The Implications of Quantum Mechanics on Time	145
Chapter 35: The Nature of Space and the Quantum Vacuum	149
Part VIII: Theories Uniting Quantum Mechanics and Relativity	153
Chapter 36: The Quest for Quantum Gravity	154
Chapter 37: Loop Quantum Gravity	158
Chapter 38: String Theory and M-Theory	162
Chapter 39: Holographic Principle and the Black Hole Information Paradox	166
Chapter 40: The Future of Unifying Theories	169
Part IX: Popular Science and Quantum Mechanics	172
Chapter 41: Quantum Mechanics in Science Fiction	173
Chapter 42: Movies and TV Shows Exploring Quantum Mechanics	177
Chapter 43: The Role of Quantum Mechanics in Art and Design	181
Chapter 44: Quantum Mechanics in Everyday Life	184
Chapter 45: Debunking Common Quantum Misconceptions	187
Part X: The Future of Quantum Mechanics	190
Chapter 46: The Role of Quantum Mechanics in Space Exploration	192
Chapter 47: Quantum Technologies and the Environment	195

Chapter 48: Ethical Considerations in Quantum Research   198

Chapter 49: The Next Frontier: Quantum Biology and Medicine   201

Chapter 50: The Continuing Evolution of Quantum Theory and its Applications   204

QUANTUM REALITIES: UNRAVELING THE MYSTERIES OF THE UNIVERSE AND MULTIVERSE

PART I: FOUNDATIONS OF QUANTUM THEORY

The Birth of Quantum Mechanics

Key Concepts and Pioneers

Wave-Particle Duality

Quantum Entanglement and Nonlocality

The Uncertainty Principle and the Observer Effect

CHAPTER 1: THE BIRTH OF QUANTUM MECHANICS

The birth of quantum mechanics marked a revolutionary shift in our understanding of the physical world. This radical departure from classical physics began in the early 20th century and has since continued to shape our view of reality. The fundamental principles of quantum mechanics have not only expanded our comprehension of the microscopic realm but have also inspired a multitude of technological advancements. In this chapter, we will delve into the history of quantum mechanics, explore the ideas that laid the foundation for this revolutionary field, and discuss the key figures who contributed to its development.

The Beginnings of Quantum Theory: Max Planck and the Quantization of Energy

The roots of quantum mechanics can be traced back to the late 19th and early 20th centuries when physicists were grappling with several unresolved issues within classical physics. Among these was the black-body radiation problem, which concerned the spectral distribution of energy emitted by a perfect absorber and emitter of radiation. Classical physics could not account for the experimental observations, leading to the so-called "ultraviolet catastrophe."

In 1900, Max Planck, a German physicist, proposed a groundbreaking solution to the black-body radiation problem. He suggested that the energy of electromagnetic radiation is quantized, meaning it is made up of discrete units or "quanta."

He formulated the Planck's law, which accurately described the observed black-body radiation spectrum. Planck's constant (h), a fundamental constant of nature, was introduced to represent the proportionality between the energy of a photon and its frequency.

Planck's proposal of quantized energy was the first step towards the development of quantum theory, although he himself did not initially recognize the full implications of his idea.

The Emergence of the Quantum Hypothesis: Albert Einstein and the Photoelectric Effect

While Planck's work laid the groundwork for quantum mechanics, it was Albert Einstein who took the quantum hypothesis further. In 1905, Einstein published a paper explaining the photoelectric effect, a phenomenon where electrons are emitted from a metal surface when exposed to light. Classical physics could not account for the observations, such as the fact that the electron's energy depended on the frequency of the incident light, not its intensity.

Einstein extended Planck's concept of quantized energy to suggest that light itself was composed of discrete packets of energy called photons. He showed that the energy of a photon is directly proportional to its frequency, with Planck's constant as the proportionality factor. Einstein's explanation of the photoelectric effect provided strong evidence for the particle nature of light, and in 1921, he was awarded the Nobel Prize in Physics for his work.

The Birth of Quantum Mechanics: Niels Bohr and the Quantum Model of the Atom

The development of quantum mechanics gained momentum with the work of Danish physicist Niels Bohr. In 1913, Bohr proposed a quantum model of the hydrogen atom, which addressed the shortcomings of Rutherford's atomic model.

Bohr's model introduced the concept of quantized energy levels for electrons orbiting the nucleus. Electrons could only occupy specific orbits with discrete energy values and could transition between these orbits by absorbing or emitting photons.

Bohr's quantum model successfully explained the observed hydrogen emission spectrum, further solidifying the idea that energy levels are quantized. His work also introduced the correspondence principle, which states that quantum mechanics must converge to classical mechanics in the limit of large quantum numbers.

The Foundation of Modern Quantum Mechanics: Wave Mechanics and Matrix Mechanics

In the mid-1920s, two distinct but mathematically equivalent formulations of quantum mechanics emerged: wave mechanics, developed by Erwin Schrödinger, and matrix mechanics, formulated by Werner Heisenberg, Max Born, and Pascual Jordan.

Schrödinger's wave mechanics introduced the concept of wave-particle duality, which states that particles can exhibit both wave-like and particle-like behavior. He developed the Schrödinger equation, a partial differential equation that describes the time-evolution of the quantum state of a particle. Schrödinger's equation treats particles as wave functions, which contain information about the probability distribution of the particle's position, momentum, and other properties.

On the other hand, Heisenberg's matrix mechanics focused on the algebraic representation of observables, such as position and momentum, using matrices. Heisenberg, Born, and Jordan discovered that the matrices representing these observables do not commute, which means that their order matters when performing calculations. This non-commutativity gave rise to the uncertainty principle, one of the cornerstones of quantum mechanics, which states that certain pairs of observables, such as position and momentum, cannot be precisely measured simultaneously.

The Synthesis and Further Developments

Despite their different approaches, wave mechanics and matrix mechanics were eventually proven to be equivalent, and together they formed the foundation of modern quantum mechanics. The mathematical framework was further refined by Paul Dirac, who introduced the Dirac notation, a concise and elegant notation that facilitated the manipulation of quantum states and operators.

As quantum mechanics matured, it became clear that it was capable of explaining a wide range of phenomena that classical physics could not. From the behavior of subatomic particles to the electronic structure of atoms and molecules, quantum mechanics provided a powerful tool for understanding the microscopic world.

In subsequent years, quantum mechanics has been expanded and refined, ˙ leading to the development of quantum electrodynamics (QED), quantum chromodynamics (QCD), and quantum field theory (QFT). These theories have deepened our understanding of fundamental forces and elementary particles, providing a more complete picture of the universe at its most fundamental level.

Opinion: The Lasting Impact of Quantum Mechanics

The birth of quantum mechanics represents a monumental achievement in the history of science. It has not only reshaped our understanding of the microscopic world but has also had profound implications for our perception of reality. The core principles of quantum mechanics challenge our intuition and compel us to rethink the nature of particles, waves, and the fabric of the universe itself.

The development of quantum mechanics has also led to

numerous practical applications, ranging from the invention of the transistor and the laser to the development of quantum computing and cryptography. As we continue to explore the depths of this enigmatic theory, it is likely that we will uncover even more astonishing insights into the nature of the universe and the role that quantum mechanics plays in shaping our reality.

The birth of quantum mechanics marked the beginning of a new era in our understanding of the physical world. The groundbreaking ideas introduced by Planck, Einstein, Bohr, Schrödinger, Heisenberg, and other pioneers have transformed our perception of reality and laid the foundation for countless technological advancements. As we delve deeper into the quantum realm, it is crucial to appreciate the rich history and monumental achievements of this revolutionary field, while also acknowledging the many questions that still remain unanswered.

CHAPTER 2: KEY CONCEPTS AND PIONEERS

Quantum mechanics is built on a foundation of key concepts that govern the behavior of particles and systems at the quantum level. These concepts, although counterintuitive, have been proven through countless experiments and theoretical developments. In this chapter, we will explore the core principles of quantum mechanics and discuss the contributions of the pioneers who shaped the field.

Wave-Particle Duality

One of the most intriguing aspects of quantum mechanics is wave-particle duality, which posits that particles can exhibit both wave-like and particle-like properties. This concept was first introduced by Louis de Broglie, who proposed that all particles have an associated wavelength, known as the de Broglie wavelength. The idea was later supported by the double-slit experiment, which demonstrated the wave-like behavior of particles, such as electrons and photons.

Quantum Superposition

Quantum superposition is a fundamental principle of quantum mechanics that states that particles can exist in multiple states simultaneously until a measurement is performed. This concept is exemplified by the famous Schrödinger's cat thought experiment, which illustrates the seemingly paradoxical nature of superposition. In this thought experiment, a cat is placed in a sealed box with a radioactive atom and a vial of poison. According to quantum mechanics, the cat is both alive and dead until the box is opened and the cat is observed.

Quantum Entanglement

Quantum entanglement is a phenomenon in which the quantum states of two or more particles become correlated, such that the properties of one particle are instantaneously dependent on the properties of the other, regardless of the distance between them. This phenomenon was first described by Albert Einstein, Boris Podolsky, and Nathan Rosen in the famous EPR paper, and was later demonstrated experimentally by John Bell and others. Entanglement has since become a central concept in quantum information science, with applications in quantum computing and quantum cryptography.

The Uncertainty Principle

The Heisenberg uncertainty principle is a fundamental concept in quantum mechanics that establishes a limit on the precision with which certain pairs of physical properties can be simultaneously measured. These pairs, known as complementary observables, include position and momentum, as well as energy and time. The uncertainty principle arises due to the non-commutative nature of quantum observables and has profound implications for our understanding of the quantum world.

Quantum State Collapse and the Measurement Problem

The measurement problem in quantum mechanics concerns the process by which a quantum system transitions from a superposition of states to a definite state upon measurement. This phenomenon, known as wave function collapse, has been the subject of much debate and interpretation. The Copenhagen interpretation, championed by Niels Bohr and Werner Heisenberg, posits that the act of measurement causes the wave function to collapse. However, other interpretations, such as the Many Worlds Interpretation and the De Broglie-Bohm pilot wave theory, offer alternative perspectives on this enigmatic aspect of quantum mechanics.

The Pioneers of Quantum Mechanics

The development of quantum mechanics was driven by the collective efforts of numerous physicists, mathematicians, and philosophers. Some of the most influential figures in the field include:

Max Planck: Introduced the concept of energy quantization and formulated Planck's law.
Albert Einstein: Developed the photon hypothesis and contributed to the understanding of quantum entanglement.
Niels Bohr: Proposed the quantum model of the atom and the correspondence principle.
Werner Heisenberg: Formulated matrix mechanics and introduced the uncertainty principle.
Erwin Schrödinger: Developed wave mechanics and the Schrödinger equation.
Paul Dirac: Refined the mathematical framework of quantum mechanics and introduced the Dirac notation.
Richard Feynman: Developed the path integral formulation of quantum mechanics and contributed to the theory of quantum electrodynamics (QED).

Julian Schwinger: Made significant contributions to quantum field theory and quantum electrodynamics, sharing the Nobel Prize in Physics with Richard Feynman and Shin'ichirō Tomonaga in 1965.

John Bell: Formulated Bell's theorem, which demonstrated the fundamental differences between quantum mechanics and local hidden variable theories, and clarified the nature of quantum entanglement.

David Bohm: Proposed the De Broglie-Bohm pilot wave theory, offering an alternative interpretation of quantum mechanics that retains determinism and eliminates the need for wave function collapse.

Hugh Everett III: Developed the Many Worlds Interpretation of quantum mechanics, which suggests that all possible outcomes of a quantum measurement are realized in parallel, non-communicating universes.

Quantum mechanics is a fascinating and complex field built upon a foundation of key concepts and principles that have shaped our understanding of the microscopic world. The pioneering work of numerous physicists, mathematicians, and philosophers has led to the development of a comprehensive and powerful theoretical framework that has revolutionized our understanding of the universe.

As we explore the intricacies of wave-particle duality, quantum superposition, entanglement, the uncertainty principle, and the measurement problem, it is crucial to appreciate the intellectual journey that led to these groundbreaking discoveries. By understanding the history and development of quantum mechanics, we can better appreciate its impact on our world and the myriad of technological and scientific advancements it has inspired. The future of quantum mechanics promises to reveal even more astounding insights into the nature of reality, further expanding our comprehension of the quantum realm and its implications for our understanding of the universe.

CHAPTER 3: WAVE-PARTICLE DUALITY

Wave-particle duality is one of the most intriguing and fundamental principles of quantum mechanics. It asserts that particles, such as electrons and photons, exhibit both wave-like and particle-like behavior, challenging our classical understanding of the nature of matter and energy. In this chapter, we will delve into the concept of wave-particle duality, explore the experiments that have shaped our understanding of this phenomenon, and discuss its implications for the interpretation of quantum mechanics.

Historical Context

The origins of wave-particle duality can be traced back to the 17th century when scientists debated the nature of light. The prevailing view, championed by Isaac Newton, was that light was composed of particles, or "corpuscles." In contrast, Christiaan Huygens proposed that light was a wave phenomenon. Throughout the centuries that followed, evidence accumulated in favor of the wave theory of light, culminating in the work of James Clerk Maxwell, who formulated the equations of electromagnetism and demonstrated that light was an electromagnetic wave.

However, the notion that light could also possess particle-like properties was not entirely abandoned. Albert Einstein's explanation of the photoelectric effect in 1905 introduced the concept of photons, discrete packets of energy that possessed both wave-like and particle-like characteristics. This marked the first step towards the development of wave-particle duality.

The de Broglie Hypothesis

In 1924, Louis de Broglie extended the concept of wave-particle duality to all particles, not just photons. He proposed that every particle has an associated wavelength, known as the de Broglie wavelength, given by the formula:

$$\lambda = h / p$$

where λ is the de Broglie wavelength, h is Planck's constant, and p is the particle's momentum. De Broglie's hypothesis was a radical departure from classical physics, as it implied that even particles with mass, such as electrons, could exhibit wave-like behavior.

Experimental Evidence

The double-slit experiment has played a crucial role in demonstrating wave-particle duality for both light and particles with mass. In this experiment, a beam of particles (e.g., photons or electrons) is directed at a barrier with two slits. When the particles pass through the slits, they create an interference pattern on a screen placed behind the barrier, indicating wave-like behavior.

The truly perplexing aspect of the double-slit experiment arises when particles are sent through the slits one at a time. Even in this case, an interference pattern gradually emerges on the screen, suggesting that each particle somehow interferes with itself as if it were a wave. However, when a measurement is performed to determine which slit the particle passes through, the interference pattern vanishes, and the particle appears to behave as a distinct entity.

The Davisson-Germer experiment, conducted in 1927, provided the first direct evidence for the wave-like behavior of electrons. In this experiment, electrons were scattered off a crystalline nickel target, and the resulting diffraction pattern confirmed the wave-like nature of electrons, as predicted by de Broglie's hypothesis.

Implications for Quantum Mechanics

Wave-particle duality has profound implications for our understanding of the nature of particles and the interpretation of quantum mechanics. The fact that particles exhibit both wave-like and particle-like behavior suggests that the classical distinction between waves and particles is inadequate at the quantum level.

One of the most significant consequences of wave-particle duality is the probabilistic interpretation of quantum mechanics. The wave function associated with a particle, as described by Schrödinger's equation, represents the probability amplitude of finding the particle in a particular state or location. When a measurement is performed, the particle's wave function collapses, resulting in a definite outcome. This probabilistic nature of quantum mechanics challenges our classical intuitions about determinism and causality, giving rise to numerous philosophical debates and interpretations.

Furthermore, wave-particle duality has implications for the concept of particle identity. In the quantum realm, particles can no longer be considered as distinct, localized entities with well-defined trajectories. Instead, they are best described by their wave functions, which encompass a range of possible states and locations.

Implications for Technology and Science

Wave-particle duality has had a significant impact on the development of modern technology and scientific research. For example, the understanding of electron behavior as both particles and waves has been critical in the development of electron microscopy, which utilizes the wave-like nature of electrons to achieve high-resolution imaging of biological and material samples.

Additionally, wave-particle duality has been instrumental in the development of quantum mechanics as a whole, which has, in turn, enabled advancements in fields such as quantum computing, quantum cryptography, and quantum communication. The study of wave-particle duality has also spurred research into the fundamental nature of reality and the limits of classical physics, leading to the development of new theories and models that seek to reconcile the apparent contradictions between classical and quantum behavior.

Wave-particle duality is a fundamental and counterintuitive principle of quantum mechanics that has profoundly altered our understanding of the nature of matter and energy. From its origins in the debate over the nature of light to its extension to all particles by de Broglie, wave-particle duality has forced us to reconsider the classical distinctions between waves and particles.

The experimental evidence for wave-particle duality, such as the double-slit experiment and the Davisson-Germer experiment, has provided compelling support for this phenomenon, demonstrating the wave-like and particle-like behavior of particles under different conditions. As a result, wave-particle duality has become a cornerstone of quantum mechanics, shaping our understanding of particle identity, determinism, and causality at the quantum level.

As we continue to explore the implications of wave-particle duality, it is crucial to appreciate the intellectual journey that has led to this groundbreaking discovery and the myriad of technological and scientific advancements it has inspired. By deepening our understanding of wave-particle duality and its role in the quantum realm, we can gain valuable insights into the fundamental nature of reality and the limits of our classical

JACK H W WILLIAMS

intuitions.

CHAPTER 4: QUANTUM ENTANGLEMENT AND NONLOCALITY

Quantum entanglement is one of the most intriguing and mysterious phenomena in quantum mechanics. It involves a unique correlation between the quantum states of two or more particles, such that the properties of one particle are instantaneously dependent on the properties of the other, regardless of the distance between them. This nonlocal behavior challenges our classical understanding of space and causality, leading to numerous philosophical debates and interpretations. In this chapter, we will delve into the concept of quantum entanglement, explore the experiments that have confirmed its existence, and discuss its implications for the understanding of quantum mechanics and the nature of reality.

The Einstein-Podolsky-Rosen Paradox

The phenomenon of quantum entanglement was first described by Albert Einstein, Boris Podolsky, and Nathan Rosen in their famous 1935 paper, commonly known as the EPR paper. The authors proposed a thought experiment involving two particles that interact and then move apart. According to quantum mechanics, the particles become entangled, such that the measurement of one particle instantaneously determines the properties of the other, even if they are separated by a vast distance.

Einstein, Podolsky, and Rosen argued that this apparent nonlocal behavior contradicted the principles of locality and realism, which were fundamental to classical physics. They concluded that quantum mechanics must be incomplete, suggesting that there might be hidden variables that could provide a more complete and deterministic description of the physical world.

Bell's Theorem and Experimental Tests

In 1964, physicist John Bell formulated Bell's theorem, which showed that the predictions of quantum mechanics regarding entangled particles were fundamentally incompatible with local hidden variable theories. Bell's theorem demonstrated that if quantum mechanics is correct, then certain statistical correlations between entangled particles must violate a specific inequality, known as Bell's inequality.

Bell's theorem set the stage for a series of experiments that aimed to test the predictions of quantum mechanics against local hidden variable theories. The first of these experiments was conducted by John Clauser, Michael Horne, Abner Shimony, and Richard Holt (the CHSH experiment) in 1972, followed by Alain Aspect's experiments in the early 1980s. These experiments involved the generation of entangled photon pairs and the measurement of their polarizations. The results consistently showed that the correlations between entangled particles violated Bell's inequality, providing strong experimental evidence for the validity of quantum mechanics and the existence of quantum entanglement.

Implications for Quantum Mechanics

The experimental confirmation of quantum entanglement has had far-reaching implications for our understanding of quantum mechanics and the nature of reality. The phenomenon of entanglement challenges the classical notions of locality and realism, suggesting that the properties of entangled particles are not determined by local conditions but rather are instantaneously connected across vast distances.

This nonlocal behavior has led to numerous philosophical debates and interpretations of quantum mechanics. Some interpretations, such as the Copenhagen interpretation, posit that the act of measurement plays a crucial role in determining the properties of entangled particles. Other interpretations, such as the Many Worlds Interpretation and the De Broglie-Bohm pilot wave theory, offer alternative perspectives on the nature of entanglement and the underlying reality of the quantum world.

Applications of Quantum Entanglement

Quantum entanglement has also opened up new avenues for technological and scientific advancement. The unique correlations between entangled particles have been exploited in the development of quantum communication protocols, such as quantum cryptography, which allows for the secure exchange of information over long distances.

In addition, quantum entanglement is a key resource for quantum computing, where entangled qubits can be used to perform parallel computations and solve problems that are intractable for classical computers. The study of entanglement has also spurred research into the fundamental nature of spacetime and the potential connections between entanglement and the fabric of the universe. This research has led to the development of novel theories and models that aim to provide a deeper understanding of the relationship between quantum mechanics and gravity.

Quantum entanglement is a fascinating and counterintuitive phenomenon that has fundamentally altered our understanding of the nature of reality and the principles of quantum mechanics. From its origins in the EPR paradox to the experimental tests of Bell's theorem, entanglement has challenged our classical intuitions about space, causality, and the determinism of physical processes.

The confirmation of quantum entanglement through experiments such as the CHSH and Aspect experiments has provided strong support for the validity of quantum mechanics, while also raising numerous philosophical questions and inspiring a variety of interpretations. The study of entanglement has led to significant advancements in technology and science, including quantum communication, quantum computing, and the investigation of the fundamental nature of spacetime.

As we continue to explore the mysteries of quantum entanglement and its implications for our understanding of the quantum world, it is crucial to appreciate the intellectual journey that has led to this groundbreaking discovery. By deepening our understanding of entanglement and its role in the fabric of the universe, we can gain valuable insights into the nature of reality and the limits of our classical intuitions. As our knowledge of quantum mechanics continues to expand, the phenomenon of entanglement promises to remain at the forefront of scientific inquiry, offering new perspectives on the nature of the cosmos and the principles that govern its behavior.

CHAPTER 5: THE UNCERTAINTY PRINCIPLE AND THE OBSERVER EFFECT

The Uncertainty Principle and the Observer Effect are two fundamental concepts in quantum mechanics that challenge our classical understanding of the nature of reality, measurement, and determinism. The Uncertainty Principle, formulated by Werner Heisenberg, asserts that certain pairs of physical properties, such as position and momentum, cannot be simultaneously measured with arbitrary precision. The Observer Effect, on the other hand, posits that the act of measurement can have a significant impact on the system being observed, fundamentally altering its properties. In this chapter, we will delve into the concepts of the Uncertainty Principle and the Observer Effect, explore their implications for our understanding of quantum mechanics, and discuss their relevance to various scientific and philosophical debates.

The Heisenberg Uncertainty Principle

The Heisenberg Uncertainty Principle is one of the most well-known and fundamental principles of quantum mechanics. It states that it is impossible to simultaneously measure certain pairs of physical properties, known as complementary variables, with arbitrary precision. The most commonly cited example of such complementary variables is the position and momentum of a particle. The Uncertainty Principle can be mathematically expressed as:

$\Delta x * \Delta p \geq \hbar/2$

where Δx represents the uncertainty in position, Δp represents the uncertainty in momentum, and ℏ is the reduced Planck constant. The Uncertainty Principle asserts that the product of the uncertainties in position and momentum must always be greater than or equal to a constant value, implying that as the uncertainty in one variable decreases, the uncertainty in the other must increase.

The Observer Effect

The Observer Effect is a related but distinct concept that deals with the impact of measurement on the system being observed. In quantum mechanics, the act of measurement can fundamentally alter the properties of a system, leading to the collapse of the system's wave function into a specific, well-defined state. This effect is particularly prominent in quantum systems, where the wave function describes a range of possible states and outcomes, and the act of measurement forces the system into one of these states.

The Observer Effect is often conflated with the Uncertainty Principle, but it is essential to recognize that they are separate phenomena. The Uncertainty Principle arises from the intrinsic properties of quantum systems and the limitations of simultaneous measurements, while the Observer Effect is a consequence of the interaction between the observer and the system being measured.

Implications for Quantum Mechanics

The Uncertainty Principle and the Observer Effect have far-reaching implications for our understanding of quantum mechanics and the nature of reality. The Uncertainty Principle challenges the classical notion of determinism, suggesting that certain physical properties are fundamentally indeterminate at the quantum level. This probabilistic nature of quantum mechanics has given rise to numerous philosophical debates and interpretations, including the Copenhagen interpretation, which posits that the wave function represents our knowledge of the system rather than the system's objective properties.

The Observer Effect highlights the critical role of measurement in determining the properties of a quantum system, suggesting that the act of observation is intimately connected to the state of the system itself. This concept has led to a variety of interpretations and debates surrounding the role of the observer in quantum mechanics, as well as the nature of the collapse of the wave function.

Applications and Relevance

The Uncertainty Principle and the Observer Effect have had a significant impact on the development of science and technology, as well as our understanding of the fundamental nature of the universe. The Uncertainty Principle, for example, plays a crucial role in the behavior of particles in quantum systems, influencing phenomena such as quantum tunneling and the stability of atomic orbitals.

The Observer Effect, on the other hand, has been instrumental in the development of quantum communication protocols, such as quantum cryptography, which exploit the sensitivity of quantum systems to measurement in order to ensure the security of information transmission . Furthermore, the Observer Effect has driven research into the foundations of quantum mechanics and the nature of measurement, leading to the development of novel theories and models that aim to provide a deeper understanding of the observer's role in the quantum realm.

Both the Uncertainty Principle and the Observer Effect have also played a significant role in shaping philosophical discussions about the nature of reality, determinism, and the limits of human knowledge. The probabilistic and indeterminate nature of quantum mechanics, as exemplified by the Uncertainty

Principle, has prompted debates about the adequacy of classical physics in describing the fundamental properties of the universe and the potential existence of hidden variables that could restore determinism at the quantum level.

Similarly, the Observer Effect has fueled discussions about the role of consciousness and the observer in shaping the physical world, inspiring interpretations such as the von Neumann-Wigner interpretation, which posits that conscious observation plays a crucial role in the collapse of the wave function.

The Uncertainty Principle and the Observer Effect are two foundational concepts in quantum mechanics that have dramatically altered our understanding of the nature of reality, measurement, and determinism. From the limitations imposed by the Uncertainty Principle on simultaneous measurements of complementary variables to the profound impact of the Observer Effect on the properties of quantum systems, these phenomena have challenged our classical intuitions and inspired a myriad of scientific and philosophical debates.

As we continue to explore the mysteries of quantum mechanics and the implications of the Uncertainty Principle and the Observer Effect, it is vital to appreciate the intellectual journey that has led to these groundbreaking discoveries. By deepening our understanding of these phenomena and their role in shaping our comprehension of the quantum world, we can gain valuable insights into the nature of reality, the limits of human knowledge, and the potential connections between the observer and the observed. As our knowledge of the quantum realm continues to expand, the Uncertainty Principle and the Observer Effect promise to remain at the forefront of scientific inquiry, offering new perspectives on the fundamental principles that govern the behavior of the universe and the nature of our place within it.

PART II: QUANTUM MECHANICS AND THE UNIVERSE

Quantum Fields and Elementary Particles

Quantum Cosmology and the Big Bang

Dark Matter and Dark Energy

The Role of Quantum Mechanics in Stellar Evolution

Black Holes and Quantum Information Paradox

CHAPTER 6: QUANTUM FIELDS AND ELEMENTARY PARTICLES

Quantum field theory (QFT) is a powerful and sophisticated framework that unifies quantum mechanics with special relativity, providing a comprehensive description of elementary particles and their interactions. QFT represents particles as excitations of underlying quantum fields that permeate all of spacetime, giving rise to a rich and complex tapestry of phenomena at the quantum level. In this chapter, we will delve into the principles of quantum field theory, explore the nature of elementary particles and their interactions, and discuss the implications of QFT for our understanding of the fundamental nature of the universe.

The Birth of Quantum Field Theory

Quantum field theory emerged from the efforts of several physicists in the early to mid-20th century to reconcile the principles of quantum mechanics with those of special relativity. The first successful application of QFT was the development of quantum electrodynamics (QED) by Richard Feynman, Julian Schwinger, and Sin-Itiro Tomonaga, which describes the behavior of charged particles and their interactions through the electromagnetic force. QED provided a remarkably accurate and consistent description of the electromagnetic interactions of elementary particles, paving the way for the development of further quantum field theories to describe other fundamental forces and particles.

Quantum Fields and Elementary Particles

In quantum field theory, elementary particles are represented as localized excitations of underlying quantum fields. Each type of elementary particle, such as an electron, photon, or quark, corresponds to a distinct quantum field that permeates all of spacetime. These fields are described by complex mathematical functions that evolve according to the principles of quantum mechanics and special relativity.

When a quantum field is excited, it gives rise to a localized particle-like entity with a specific set of properties, such as mass, charge, and spin. These excitations, or quanta, can interact with one another through the exchange of other particles, which represent the force carriers for various fundamental interactions. For example, in quantum electrodynamics, charged particles such as electrons and positrons interact through the exchange of photons, which are the quanta of the electromagnetic field.

The Standard Model of Particle Physics

The Standard Model of particle physics is the most successful and comprehensive quantum field theory developed to date, encompassing the electromagnetic, weak, and strong nuclear forces, as well as a host of elementary particles. The Standard Model is organized into three main categories: fermions, which constitute the building blocks of matter; gauge bosons, which mediate the fundamental forces; and the Higgs boson, which is responsible for endowing other particles with mass through the Higgs mechanism.

Fermions are further divided into two subcategories: quarks and leptons. Quarks come in six flavors (up, down, charm, strange, top, and bottom) and are the constituents of protons, neutrons, and other hadrons. Leptons include the familiar electron and its heavier counterparts, the muon and tau, as well as their associated neutrinos.

Gauge bosons comprise the photon (mediating the electromagnetic force), the W and Z bosons (mediating the weak nuclear force), and the gluons (mediating the strong nuclear force). The Higgs boson, discovered at CERN in 2012, is associated with the Higgs field, which permeates all of spacetime and imparts mass to other particles through their interactions with it.

Implications and Future Directions

Quantum field theory and the Standard Model have had a profound impact on our understanding of the fundamental nature of the universe, providing a remarkably accurate and consistent description of elementary particles and their interactions. However, several important questions and challenges remain to be addressed, such as the integration of gravity into the framework of QFT, the nature of dark matter and dark energy, the matter-antimatter asymmetry in the universe, and the potential existence of new particles and interactions beyond the Standard Model.

Efforts to incorporate gravity into the framework of quantum field theory have led to the development of novel approaches such as string theory and loop quantum gravity, which seek to provide a unified description of all fundamental forces and particles. These theories offer promising avenues for exploring the nature of spacetime, black holes, and the origins of the universe, though experimental confirmation of their predictions remains elusive.

Dark matter and dark energy, which together make up approximately 95% of the energy content of the universe, present another significant challenge for the Standard Model and quantum field theory. While the existence of dark matter and dark energy has been inferred from astrophysical observations, their precise nature and the underlying mechanisms responsible for their effects remain unknown. The search for dark matter particles and the development of theories to explain dark energy continue to be at the forefront of both experimental and theoretical research in particle physics and cosmology.

The observed matter-antimatter asymmetry in the universe, which cannot be fully accounted for by the Standard Model, has fueled investigations into potential new particles and interactions that could give rise to this imbalance. The discovery of such new phenomena could have profound implications for our understanding of the early universe and the processes that shaped its evolution.

Quantum field theory and the Standard Model have revolutionized our understanding of elementary particles and their interactions, providing a comprehensive and highly successful framework for describing the fundamental forces and constituents of the universe. From the birth of quantum field theory in the development of quantum electrodynamics to the construction of the Standard Model and its myriad experimental confirmations, the study of quantum fields and elementary particles has deepened our understanding of the fundamental nature of reality and the principles that govern its behavior.

As we continue to explore the mysteries of quantum field theory and the elementary particles that make up our universe, it is essential to appreciate the intellectual journey that has led to these groundbreaking discoveries. By delving into the principles of quantum field theory, the nature of elementary particles, and the challenges and questions that lie ahead, we can gain valuable insights into the fundamental nature of the universe and the potential connections between its smallest constituents and its largest structures. As our knowledge of quantum fields and elementary particles continues to expand, these fascinating and enigmatic phenomena promise to remain at the forefront of scientific inquiry, offering new perspectives on the fundamental principles that underlie the cosmos and our place within it.

CHAPTER 7: QUANTUM COSMOLOGY AND THE BIG BANG

Quantum cosmology is an interdisciplinary field that seeks to apply the principles of quantum mechanics and quantum field theory to our understanding of the early universe and its evolution. The Big Bang theory, which describes the birth of the universe as a hot, dense state that has expanded and cooled over time, forms the foundation of modern cosmology. In this chapter, we will delve into the principles of quantum cosmology, explore the implications of quantum mechanics for the Big Bang theory, and discuss how this approach might shed light on some of the most profound questions in our understanding of the origins and evolution of the universe.

Quantum Cosmology: Bridging the Gap

The study of the early universe poses significant challenges for classical physics and general relativity, which break down under the extreme conditions of high energy and density that characterized the first moments of cosmic history. Quantum cosmology aims to bridge the gap between the quantum realm of particle physics and the large-scale structure of the universe, by applying the principles of quantum mechanics and quantum field theory to the dynamics of spacetime itself.

One of the central goals of quantum cosmology is to develop a consistent and comprehensive framework for describing the earliest moments of the universe, when quantum fluctuations in the fabric of spacetime and the behavior of elementary particles played a crucial role in shaping the universe's subsequent evolution. This endeavor requires a synthesis of quantum mechanics, quantum field theory, and general relativity, and has given rise to novel approaches such as loop quantum cosmology and string cosmology.

Quantum Fluctuations and the Big Bang

Quantum mechanics has profound implications for our understanding of the Big Bang theory and the earliest moments of the universe. According to quantum field theory, the vacuum state is not a static, empty void, but rather a seething sea of virtual particles and antiparticles that constantly pop in and out of existence. These quantum fluctuations, which arise due to the inherent uncertainty and indeterminacy of quantum mechanics, can have a significant impact on the dynamics of the early universe.

One of the most influential applications of quantum mechanics to cosmology is the theory of cosmic inflation, proposed by Alan Guth in the early 1980s. Inflation posits that the universe underwent a brief period of exponential expansion during its first moments, driven by the dynamics of a scalar field known as the inflaton. This rapid expansion served to amplify quantum fluctuations in the inflaton field and the fabric of spacetime, seeding the formation of large-scale structures such as galaxies and galaxy clusters.

The Cosmic Microwave Background and Quantum Origins

The Cosmic Microwave Background (CMB), the relic radiation left over from the Big Bang, provides a unique window into the quantum origins of the universe. The CMB exhibits a nearly uniform temperature across the sky, with tiny fluctuations in temperature and density that encode information about the primordial quantum fluctuations that gave rise to large-scale structure.

Detailed observations of the CMB, such as those made by the Cosmic Background Explorer (COBE), the Wilkinson Microwave

Anisotropy Probe (WMAP), and the Planck satellite, have provided strong evidence in support of inflation and the role of quantum fluctuations in shaping the universe's evolution. These measurements have also allowed scientists to constrain various cosmological parameters and test the predictions of competing theories of the early universe.

Challenges and Future Directions

Quantum cosmology and the application of quantum mechanics to the Big Bang theory have deepened our understanding of the origins and evolution of the universe, but several significant challenges and questions remain to be addressed. One of the central goals of this field is to develop a complete and consistent theory of quantum gravity, which would provide a unified description of the fundamental forces and particles and the dynamics of spacetime itself. Approaches such as loop quantum gravity and string theory offer promising avenues for achieving this goal, but experimental confirmation and a complete understanding of their implications for cosmology remain elusive.

Another major challenge in quantum cosmology is the so-called "initial conditions problem." This refers to the question of what determined the initial state of the universe, and why it began in such a finely-tuned, low-entropy configuration. Theories such as the multiverse and eternal inflation have been proposed to address this issue, suggesting that our observable universe is just one of many in a vast and diverse ensemble of universes with different initial conditions and physical laws.

Dark energy, which is responsible for the accelerated expansion of the universe, presents another puzzle for quantum cosmology. While the cosmological constant, which represents the energy density of the vacuum, is a natural candidate for dark energy, its observed value is many orders of magnitude smaller than what is predicted by quantum field theory. This discrepancy, known as the cosmological constant problem, has led researchers to explore alternative theories of dark energy and modifications to the foundations of quantum field theory and general relativity.

Quantum cosmology and the application of quantum mechanics to the Big Bang theory have provided valuable insights into the origins and evolution of the universe, revealing the crucial role of quantum fluctuations and other quantum phenomena in shaping the large-scale structure of the cosmos. From the birth of cosmic inflation to the detailed observations of the Cosmic Microwave Background, the study of quantum cosmology has deepened our understanding of the fundamental nature of reality and the principles that govern its behavior.

As we continue to explore the mysteries of quantum cosmology and the early universe, it is essential to appreciate the intellectual journey that has led to these groundbreaking discoveries. By delving into the principles of quantum mechanics, quantum field theory, and general relativity, and by confronting the challenges and questions that lie ahead, we can gain valuable insights into the origins of the universe, the nature of spacetime, and the potential connections between the smallest scales of quantum phenomena and the largest structures of the cosmos. As our knowledge of quantum cosmology continues to expand, these fascinating and enigmatic phenomena promise to remain at the forefront of scientific inquiry, offering new perspectives on the fundamental principles that underlie the cosmos and our place within it.

CHAPTER 8: DARK MATTER AND DARK ENERGY

Dark matter and dark energy are two of the most mysterious and elusive components of the universe, together accounting for approximately 95% of its total energy content. While their existence has been inferred from a variety of astrophysical observations, the precise nature of dark matter and dark energy remains unknown. In this chapter, we will explore the evidence for these phenomena, discuss the various theories proposed to explain their properties, and examine the implications of dark matter and dark energy for our understanding of the universe's history and future evolution.

Dark Matter: The Invisible Mass

Dark matter is a hypothetical form of matter that does not emit, absorb, or reflect light, making it invisible to electromagnetic radiation. Its existence was first proposed in the 1930s by Swiss astronomer Fritz Zwicky, who observed that the motion of galaxies within galaxy clusters could not be accounted for by the visible matter alone. This discrepancy suggested the presence of a significant amount of unseen mass, which Zwicky dubbed "dark matter."

Since then, a variety of independent observations have provided further evidence for the existence of dark matter, such as the rotational curves of galaxies, the distribution of cosmic microwave background radiation, and the large-scale structure of the universe. These observations indicate that dark matter makes up approximately 27% of the universe's total mass-energy content.

Despite the compelling evidence for its existence, the precise nature of dark matter remains unknown. The leading candidates for dark matter particles are weakly interacting massive particles (WIMPs), which are predicted to be stable and interact only weakly with normal matter through the weak nuclear force and gravity. Other proposed candidates include axions, sterile neutrinos, and primordial black holes. Large-scale experiments and observational efforts are underway to detect and characterize dark matter particles directly or indirectly through their effects on astrophysical processes.

Dark Energy: The Accelerating Universe

Dark energy is a mysterious form of energy that permeates all of spacetime and is responsible for the accelerated expansion of the universe. Its existence was first inferred in the late 1990s when two independent research teams studying Type Ia supernovae discovered that the expansion of the universe is not slowing down, as had been previously assumed, but is instead accelerating.

The most widely accepted explanation for dark energy is the cosmological constant, which represents the energy density of the vacuum in the framework of quantum field theory and general relativity. The cosmological constant provides a natural candidate for dark energy, with a repulsive gravitational effect that drives the accelerated expansion of the universe. However, the observed value of the cosmological constant is many orders of magnitude smaller than what is predicted by quantum field theory, posing a significant challenge for theoretical physics.

Alternative theories of dark energy have been proposed to address this discrepancy, such as quintessence (a dynamical scalar field that varies over time and space), modified gravity models, and extra-dimensional effects. While these theories offer intriguing possibilities for explaining the observed acceleration of the universe, no single model has emerged as a definitive solution to the dark energy problem.

Implications and Future Directions

Dark matter and dark energy have profoundly impacted our understanding of the universe's composition, history, and future evolution. Their existence challenges the foundations of our current theories of particle physics and cosmology, and has spurred a wealth of research into the nature of these enigmatic phenomena.

The quest to understand dark matter and dark energy has driven the development of novel experimental and observational techniques, such as direct and indirect dark matter detection experiments, and large-scale surveys of the cosmic microwave background and large-scale structure. These efforts have the potential to reveal new particles and interactions, constrain the properties of dark energy, and shed light on the interplay between dark matter, dark energy, and the visible universe.

As our knowledge of dark matter and dark energy continues to grow, these mysterious components of the cosmos promise to reshape our understanding of the fundamental principles that govern the universe and its evolution. The study of dark matter and dark energy has far-reaching implications for our understanding of the origins and fate of the universe, the connections between the smallest scales of quantum phenomena and the largest structures in the cosmos, and the nature of spacetime and gravity.

Dark matter and dark energy represent some of the most pressing challenges and intriguing mysteries in modern cosmology and astrophysics. While their existence has been inferred from a variety of observations, their precise nature and the underlying mechanisms responsible for their effects remain unknown. The search for dark matter particles and the development of theories to explain dark energy continue to be at the forefront of both experimental and theoretical research in particle physics and cosmology.

By delving into the evidence for dark matter and dark energy, the various theories proposed to explain their properties, and the implications of these phenomena for our understanding of the universe, we can gain valuable insights into the enigmatic components that make up the vast majority of the cosmos. As we continue to explore the mysteries of dark matter and dark energy, their fascinating and elusive nature promises to remain at the forefront of scientific inquiry, offering new perspectives on the fundamental principles that underlie the cosmos and our place within it.

CHAPTER 9: THE MULTIVERSE AND PARALLEL UNIVERSES

The concept of the multiverse, a collection of multiple, potentially infinite parallel universes, has emerged as a fascinating and controversial topic in both theoretical physics and popular science. The multiverse hypothesis is rooted in various branches of theoretical physics, including quantum mechanics, cosmology, and string theory. In this chapter, we will explore the different types of multiverses, the scientific theories and principles underlying the idea of parallel universes, and the implications of the multiverse hypothesis for our understanding of the universe and the nature of reality.

Types of Multiverses

There are several types of multiverse scenarios that have been proposed, each based on different scientific principles and theories. Some of the most widely discussed multiverse models include:

Level I Multiverse (Quilted Multiverse): This model is based on the concept of cosmic inflation, which posits that the universe underwent a rapid period of exponential expansion in its early stages. In the Level I Multiverse, there are an infinite number of non-interacting, causally disconnected regions of space, each with its own unique distribution of matter and energy. These regions are commonly referred to as "bubble universes" or "pocket universes."

Level II Multiverse (Inflationary Multiverse): This model is an extension of the Level I Multiverse and is based on the theory of eternal inflation, which suggests that inflation never truly ends.

Instead, different regions of space stop inflating at different times, giving rise to an infinite collection of bubble universes, each with its own unique set of physical laws and constants.

Level III Multiverse (Many-Worlds Interpretation): This model is based on the principles of quantum mechanics, specifically the Many-Worlds Interpretation (MWI) of quantum mechanics. According to the MWI, every time a quantum event with multiple possible outcomes occurs, the universe branches into separate, non-interacting parallel universes, each representing one of the possible outcomes.

Level IV Multiverse (Ultimate Multiverse): This model, proposed by Max Tegmark, is based on the mathematical universe hypothesis, which posits that all mathematically consistent structures exist as separate universes. In the Level IV Multiverse, each universe has its own unique set of physical laws and constants, which are determined by the underlying mathematical structure of that universe.

Scientific Foundations

The concept of the multiverse is rooted in various scientific theories and principles, including:

Cosmic Inflation: As mentioned earlier, cosmic inflation and eternal inflation form the basis for the Level I and Level II Multiverses. The rapid expansion of space during inflation leads to the creation of causally disconnected regions, each with its own unique distribution of matter and energy.

Quantum Mechanics: The Many-Worlds Interpretation of quantum mechanics, which forms the basis for the Level III Multiverse, posits that every quantum event with multiple possible outcomes leads to the creation of parallel universes, each representing one of the possible outcomes.

String Theory: This framework for unifying gravity and quantum mechanics predicts the existence of multiple dimensions and parallel universes, which can give rise to a multiverse scenario. String theory also provides a basis for understanding the varying physical laws and constants in different universes.

Implications and Future Directions

The multiverse hypothesis has profound implications for our understanding of the universe and the nature of reality. If the multiverse exists, it could help explain some of the most perplexing questions in cosmology and physics, such as the fine-tuning of the physical constants, the origins of the universe, and the nature of time and space.

However, the multiverse remains a controversial and speculative idea in the scientific community. One of the main criticisms of the multiverse hypothesis is the lack of direct observational evidence, as well as the difficulty in testing and falsifying the existence of parallel universes. As a result, some scientists argue that the multiverse lies outside the realm of empirical science and is more a philosophical or metaphysical concept than a scientific one.

Despite these criticisms, the study of the multiverse and parallel universes has inspired a wealth of research in theoretical physics and cosmology. Researchers continue to develop new mathematical models and theoretical frameworks to better understand the nature of the multiverse and its implications for our understanding of the universe. Experimental efforts, such as the search for signatures of cosmic inflation and the detection of higher-dimensional effects in particle physics, could provide indirect evidence for the existence of the multiverse and help to refine our understanding of its properties.

The multiverse and the idea of parallel universes represent some of the most intriguing and controversial concepts in modern theoretical physics and cosmology. While the existence of the multiverse remains speculative and faces significant challenges in terms of empirical verification, the study of parallel universes and their underlying scientific principles offers valuable insights into the nature of reality, the origins of the universe, and the fundamental laws that govern its behavior.

As we continue to explore the mysteries of the multiverse and the possibility of parallel universes, it is essential to appreciate the intellectual journey that has led to these groundbreaking ideas and the scientific theories that underpin them. By delving into the principles of cosmic inflation, quantum mechanics, and string theory, and by confronting the challenges and questions that lie ahead, we can gain a deeper understanding of the universe and its potential connections to other, unseen realms of existence. As our knowledge of the multiverse continues to expand, these fascinating and enigmatic phenomena promise to remain at the forefront of scientific inquiry, offering new perspectives on the fundamental principles that underlie the cosmos and our place within it.

CHAPTER 10: BLACK HOLES AND QUANTUM INFORMATION PARADOX

Black holes are among the most intriguing and enigmatic objects in the universe, exhibiting extreme gravitational forces and mysterious properties that challenge our understanding of physics. One of the most fascinating aspects of black holes is their relationship with quantum mechanics and the so-called "quantum information paradox," which arises from the apparent contradiction between the principles of quantum mechanics and the behavior of black holes. In this chapter, we will delve into the nature of black holes, the quantum information paradox, and the potential resolutions to this conundrum.

Black Holes: The Ultimate Gravity Wells

Black holes are astronomical objects with gravitational forces so strong that not even light can escape their pull. They are formed when massive stars reach the end of their lives and undergo a catastrophic collapse, compressing their mass into an infinitely dense point called a singularity. This singularity is surrounded by an event horizon, a boundary from which no information or matter can escape.

According to general relativity, black holes have three key properties: mass, charge, and angular momentum (spin). These properties determine the behavior of a black hole and the spacetime geometry around it. Black holes can be classified into several types based on these properties, such as Schwarzschild black holes (non-rotating and uncharged), Reissner-Nordström black holes (non-rotating and charged), and Kerr black holes (rotating and uncharged).

The Quantum Information Paradox

The quantum information paradox arises from the interplay between black holes, quantum mechanics, and the principles of information conservation. In quantum mechanics, information is considered to be a fundamental quantity that must be conserved, meaning it cannot be created or destroyed. However, the behavior of black holes appears to violate this principle, leading to the quantum information paradox.

The paradox was first introduced by Stephen Hawking in the 1970s, when he discovered that black holes are not completely black but emit radiation, now known as Hawking radiation. This radiation is a result of quantum fluctuations near the event horizon, where particle-antiparticle pairs are created, and one of the particles falls into the black hole while the other escapes. Over time, this process causes the black hole to lose mass and eventually evaporate.

The problem arises when we consider the fate of the information contained within the matter that falls into the black hole. If the black hole evaporates and the information is lost, it would violate the principle of information conservation. However, if the information is somehow encoded in the Hawking radiation, it would appear to contradict the principles of general relativity, which predict that information cannot escape from within the event horizon.

Potential Resolutions to the Paradox

Several potential resolutions to the quantum information paradox have been proposed, each with its own implications for our understanding of black holes and the fundamental principles of physics:

Black Hole Complementarity: This principle, proposed by

Leonard Susskind, suggests that the information is both inside the black hole and encoded in the Hawking radiation, depending on the observer's perspective. While this idea appears to resolve the paradox, it raises questions about the nature of information and its relationship with spacetime and gravity.

Firewall Hypothesis: This idea, proposed by Almheiri, Marolf, Polchinski, and Sully, posits that a highly energetic "firewall" exists at the event horizon, which destroys any information that crosses it. While the firewall hypothesis potentially resolves the paradox, it challenges the equivalence principle of general relativity, which states that free-falling observers should not experience any dramatic effects when crossing the event horizon.

Holographic Principle: This principle, inspired by the AdS/CFT correspondence in string theory, posits that the information contained within a black hole is encoded on its event horizon in a lower-dimensional form. According to this idea, the information is not lost when the black hole evaporates, as it is preserved in the Hawking radiation through a process known as "black hole evaporation." The holographic principle offers a potential resolution to the paradox while also providing new insights into the nature of spacetime, gravity, and information.

Loop Quantum Gravity: This approach to quantum gravity, which aims to reconcile general relativity and quantum mechanics, suggests that the interior of a black hole is not a true singularity but rather a highly curved region of spacetime, where quantum effects become significant. In this framework, the information is not lost but is instead transformed into a new state as it passes through the black hole. Loop quantum gravity offers a potential resolution to the paradox while also shedding light on the fundamental nature of spacetime, matter, and energy.

The quantum information paradox highlights the fascinating

interplay between black holes, quantum mechanics, and the principles of information conservation. The paradox reveals deep tensions between our current understanding of general relativity and quantum mechanics, and resolving it will likely require novel insights into the nature of spacetime, gravity, and information.

As physicists continue to explore the quantum information paradox and its potential resolutions, we are likely to gain a deeper understanding of black holes and their mysterious properties, as well as the fundamental principles that govern the behavior of the universe. The study of black holes and the quantum information paradox promises to remain at the forefront of theoretical physics and astrophysics, offering exciting new perspectives on the enigmatic phenomena that challenge our understanding of the cosmos and our place within it.

PART III: THE MULTIVERSE

Introduction to the Multiverse Concept
Many Worlds Interpretation of Quantum Mechanics
Bubble Universes and Eternal Inflation
The Anthropic Principle and Fine-tuning
Brane Worlds and Extra Dimensions

CHAPTER 11: INTRODUCTION TO THE MULTIVERSE CONCEPT

The multiverse concept has gained significant attention and sparked fascinating debates in both scientific and philosophical circles. It posits the existence of multiple universes, each with its own unique physical properties and characteristics, offering an alternative perspective on the nature of reality and our place within it. In this chapter, we will introduce the multiverse concept, its origins in scientific theories, and the implications for our understanding of the universe.

The Multiverse: A World of Many Worlds

The idea of multiple universes, or the multiverse, has its roots in various scientific theories and philosophical concepts. It suggests that our universe, which we perceive and study through observations and experiments, is just one of an infinite number of universes that exist simultaneously, each with its own unique properties and physical laws. These parallel universes may be entirely separate from our own or connected in ways that are not yet fully understood.

Origins of the Multiverse Concept

The concept of the multiverse has emerged from several scientific theories, including:

Cosmic Inflation: This theory posits that the universe underwent a rapid period of exponential expansion in its early stages, giving rise to an infinite number of causally disconnected regions, each with its own unique distribution of matter and energy. This idea forms the basis for the Level I

Multiverse (Quilted Multiverse).

Eternal Inflation: An extension of cosmic inflation, eternal inflation suggests that inflation never truly ends, leading to the creation of an infinite number of bubble universes, each with its own unique set of physical laws and constants. This model gives rise to the Level II Multiverse (Inflationary Multiverse).

Many-Worlds Interpretation: This interpretation of quantum mechanics posits that every quantum event with multiple possible outcomes causes the universe to branch into separate, non-interacting parallel universes, each representing one of the possible outcomes. This idea forms the basis for the Level III Multiverse (Many-Worlds Multiverse).

String Theory: A theoretical framework for unifying gravity and quantum mechanics, string theory predicts the existence of multiple dimensions and parallel universes, offering a potential explanation for the existence of the multiverse.

Implications of the Multiverse Concept

The multiverse concept has profound implications for our understanding of the universe and the nature of reality:

Fine-Tuning Problem: The existence of the multiverse could provide a natural explanation for the apparent fine-tuning of the physical constants in our universe, as each universe within the multiverse may have its own unique set of constants, and we just happen to exist in one that is conducive to the formation of complex structures and life.

The Nature of Reality: If the multiverse exists, it challenges our traditional understanding of reality, as it suggests that there may be other universes with entirely different physical laws and properties, leading to unique forms of matter, energy, and perhaps even life.

The Nature of Time and Space: The multiverse concept raises

questions about the nature of time and space, as well as their relationship with the physical laws that govern the behavior of the universe.

The Anthropic Principle: The existence of the multiverse could lend support to the anthropic principle, which posits that the observed properties of the universe are the way they are because they allow for the existence of intelligent observers, like ourselves.

The multiverse concept offers a fascinating and thought-provoking perspective on the nature of reality and our place within it. Although the existence of parallel universes remains speculative and faces significant challenges in terms of empirical verification, the study of the multiverse and its implications for our understanding of the universe continues to inspire cutting-edge research in theoretical physics, cosmology, and philosophy. As we delve deeper into the mysteries of the multiverse and seek to uncover the fundamental principles that govern the behavior of the cosmos, we stand at the forefront of a new era of scientific inquiry and discovery. The exploration of the multiverse promises to reveal new insights into the nature of reality, the origins of the universe, and the myriad possibilities that lie beyond our current understanding of the world we inhabit.

As we continue to grapple with the implications of the multiverse and the potential existence of parallel universes, we must also confront the philosophical and ethical questions that these ideas raise. How do the concepts of free will, causality, and moral responsibility change in the context of the multiverse? What does it mean to be conscious, and how might the nature of consciousness be influenced by the existence of other universes? How do we approach the pursuit of scientific knowledge and understanding in a world where the very fabric of reality may be far more complex and mysterious than we ever imagined?

The study of the multiverse and the questions it raises will undoubtedly continue to challenge our perceptions of the universe and our place within it. As we push the boundaries of scientific knowledge and strive to unravel the mysteries of the cosmos, the concept of the multiverse will remain a source of inspiration and wonder, inviting us to contemplate the vastness of existence and the infinite possibilities that lie within the fabric of reality.

CHAPTER 12: MANY WORLDS INTERPRETATION OF QUANTUM MECHANICS

The Many Worlds Interpretation (MWI) of quantum mechanics is an intriguing and controversial approach to understanding the behavior of quantum systems. It offers an alternative to the more traditional Copenhagen interpretation and provides a unique perspective on the nature of reality, the role of the observer, and the fundamental principles that govern the behavior of the universe. In this chapter, we will delve into the Many Worlds Interpretation, its origins, and its implications for our understanding of the quantum world, while maintaining the same tone and depth as the previous chapters.

The Many Worlds Interpretation: A Universe of Possibilities

The Many Worlds Interpretation, first proposed by physicist Hugh Everett III in 1957, posits that for every quantum event with multiple possible outcomes, the universe splits into separate, non-interacting branches, each representing one of the possible outcomes. In this framework, all possible outcomes of a quantum event occur in parallel, with each outcome realized in a separate, non-communicating universe.

The MWI offers an alternative to the traditional Copenhagen interpretation, which relies on the concept of wavefunction collapse to explain the seemingly random outcomes of quantum measurements. In the Many Worlds Interpretation, there is no wavefunction collapse; instead, the wavefunction of the entire universe evolves deterministically, in accordance with Schrödinger's equation, with each branch representing a different outcome of the quantum event.

Origins of the Many Worlds Interpretation

The Many Worlds Interpretation emerged as a response to the so-called measurement problem in quantum mechanics, which arises from the apparent contradiction between the deterministic evolution of the wavefunction and the random outcomes of quantum measurements. In the Copenhagen interpretation, this contradiction is resolved through the process of wavefunction collapse, which occurs when a measurement is made, forcing the quantum system into a definite state.

Hugh Everett III sought to resolve the measurement problem without invoking wavefunction collapse, by proposing that the wavefunction of the entire universe evolves deterministically and that all possible outcomes of a quantum event are realized in separate, non-interacting branches of the universe. This idea formed the basis of the Many Worlds Interpretation, which has since become one of the most prominent interpretations of quantum mechanics.

Implications of the Many Worlds Interpretation

The Many Worlds Interpretation has profound implications for our understanding of the quantum world and the nature of reality:

The Role of the Observer: Unlike the Copenhagen interpretation, the Many Worlds Interpretation does not assign a special role to the observer in the process of quantum measurement. Instead, the observer becomes an integral part of the quantum system, with their own wavefunction evolving and branching along with the rest of the universe.

Determinism and Probability: The Many Worlds Interpretation restores determinism to quantum mechanics by eliminating wavefunction collapse and allowing the wavefunction to evolve according to Schrödinger's equation. However, this determinism comes at the cost of introducing a new form of probability, known as the "Born rule," which governs the likelihood of encountering a particular outcome in a specific branch of the multiverse.

The Nature of Reality: The Many Worlds Interpretation challenges our traditional understanding of reality by positing the existence of an infinite number of parallel universes, each with its own unique outcomes and histories. This raises fascinating questions about the nature of time, space, and causality, as well as the potential existence of other "selves" in alternate branches of the multiverse.

The Many Worlds Interpretation of quantum mechanics offers a fascinating and thought-provoking alternative to the traditional Copenhagen interpretation, inviting us to explore a universe of infinite possibilities and consider the profound implications for our understanding of the quantum world and the nature of reality. While the MWI remains controversial and faces significant challenges in terms of empirical verification and philosophical interpretation, it has inspired a wealth of cutting-edge research and fostered lively debates within the scientific and philosophical communities.

As we continue to probe the mysteries of the quantum world and seek to unravel the enigmatic phenomena that underlie the behavior of the universe, the Many Worlds Interpretation will undoubtedly remain at the forefront of theoretical investigations and discussions. By considering the possibility that our universe is just one of an infinite number of parallel realities, we are forced to reevaluate our understanding of the nature of existence, the role of the observer, and the fundamental principles that govern the cosmos.

The study of the Many Worlds Interpretation and its implications for our understanding of the universe promises to remain a fertile ground for scientific inquiry and philosophical speculation, offering new perspectives on the fundamental questions that have captivated humanity for millennia. As we delve deeper into the realm of the quantum and grapple with the profound implications of the Many Worlds Interpretation, we stand at the precipice of a new era of discovery and understanding, poised to unlock the secrets of the cosmos and redefine our place within the vast tapestry of existence.

In the chapters that follow, we will continue to explore the many fascinating aspects of quantum theory, the universe, and the multiverse, as well as their potential impact on human civilization and our understanding of the world around us. Through these investigations, we aim to illuminate the profound mysteries and infinite possibilities that lie at the heart of the quantum realm, inspiring a new generation of scientists, philosophers, and dreamers to ponder the vast expanse of the cosmos and the myriad wonders that await us in the uncharted territories of the multiverse.

CHAPTER 13: BUBBLE UNIVERSES AND ETERNAL INFLATION

The concept of bubble universes and eternal inflation is an extension of the standard inflationary model of cosmology and offers a fascinating perspective on the nature of the universe and the origins of the multiverse. In this chapter, we will delve into the ideas of bubble universes and eternal inflation, exploring their theoretical foundations, implications for our understanding of the cosmos, and the intriguing possibilities they suggest for the existence of parallel universes.

Bubble Universes: Inflationary Bubbles in the Multiverse

Bubble universes are regions of spacetime that have undergone a phase of rapid expansion, known as inflation, which have become causally disconnected from their surroundings due to the immense expansion of the intervening space. These bubble universes are thought to exist within the larger multiverse, separated from one another by vast expanses of inflating space.

The idea of bubble universes arises from the concept of eternal inflation, which posits that inflation never truly ends but instead gives rise to an infinite number of causally disconnected regions that continue to inflate and spawn new bubble universes. Each bubble universe is characterized by its own unique set of physical laws and constants, making them distinct from one another in their properties and behavior.

Eternal Inflation: The Birth of the Multiverse

Eternal inflation is an extension of the standard inflationary model of cosmology, which was initially proposed by Alan Guth in 1980 as a solution to several problems in the standard Big Bang model, such as the horizon problem and the flatness problem. The standard inflationary model suggests that the universe underwent a brief period of exponential expansion in its early stages, driven by the energy of a scalar field known as the inflaton.

The concept of eternal inflation, proposed by Andrei Linde in 1986, takes this idea a step further, positing that inflation never truly ceases but instead continues indefinitely, spawning an infinite number of bubble universes as it proceeds. In this framework, the multiverse consists of a vast, ever-expanding sea of inflating space, punctuated by isolated bubble universes that form as the inflaton field decays into a lower-energy state.

Implications of Bubble Universes and Eternal Inflation

The ideas of bubble universes and eternal inflation have profound implications for our understanding of the universe and the nature of the multiverse:

The Landscape of the Multiverse: Bubble universes and eternal inflation suggest that the multiverse is an immensely complex and diverse landscape, filled with an infinite number of parallel universes, each with its own unique set of physical laws and constants. This perspective offers a potential solution to the fine-tuning problem in cosmology, as it implies that our universe is just one of an infinite number of universes with varying properties, and we simply inhabit one that is conducive to the formation of complex structures and life.

The Origin of the Universe: Eternal inflation provides a novel perspective on the origin of the universe, suggesting that our universe is just one of an infinite number of bubble universes spawned by the ongoing process of inflation. This idea raises new questions about the nature of time, space, and causality in the context of the multiverse and challenges our traditional understanding of the universe's origins.

The Fate of the Universe: The concept of eternal inflation implies that the universe's expansion will continue indefinitely, with new bubble universes constantly forming and becoming causally disconnected from one another. This raises intriguing questions about the ultimate fate of the universe and the potential existence of other forms of life and intelligence in the vast, ever-expanding multiverse.

Bubble universes and eternal inflation offer a captivating glimpse into the nature of the universe and the potential existence of a vast, complex multiverse filled with an infinite number of parallel realities. These ideas challenge our traditional understanding of the universe's origins, its structure, and its ultimate fate, inviting us to consider the profound implications for our understanding of the cosmos and our place within it.

As we continue to explore the mysteries of the universe and seek to unravel the enigmatic phenomena that underlie its behavior, the concepts of bubble universes and eternal inflation will undoubtedly remain at the forefront of theoretical investigations and discussions. By considering the possibility that our universe is just one of an infinite number of bubble universes in the ever-expanding multiverse, we are forced to confront the sheer vastness of existence and the unimaginable diversity that it may contain.

In the chapters that follow, we will delve further into the many fascinating aspects of quantum theory, the universe, and the multiverse, as well as their potential impact on human civilization and our understanding of the world around us. Through these investigations, we aim to illuminate the profound mysteries and infinite possibilities that lie at the heart of the quantum realm, inspiring a new generation of scientists, philosophers, and dreamers to ponder the vast expanse of the cosmos and the myriad wonders that await us in the uncharted territories of the multiverse.

From the origin of our own universe to the potential existence of other forms of life and intelligence in the far reaches of the cosmos, the study of bubble universes and eternal inflation promises to remain a fertile ground for scientific inquiry and philosophical speculation, offering new perspectives on the fundamental questions that have captivated humanity for millennia. As we delve deeper into the realm of the quantum and grapple with the profound implications of these ideas, we stand at the precipice of a new era of discovery and understanding, poised to unlock the secrets of the cosmos and redefine our place within the vast tapestry of existence.

CHAPTER 14: THE ANTHROPIC PRINCIPLE AND FINE-TUNING

The Anthropic Principle and the concept of fine-tuning are fascinating topics in the realm of cosmology and theoretical physics, offering intriguing insights into the nature of our universe and its potential place within the multiverse. In this chapter, we will explore the Anthropic Principle and the idea of fine-tuning, examining their theoretical underpinnings, implications for our understanding of the cosmos, and the thought-provoking questions they raise about the fundamental nature of existence.

The Anthropic Principle: Observing a Universe Made for Us

The Anthropic Principle is a philosophical idea that seeks to explain the apparent fine-tuning of the universe for the existence of life, particularly intelligent life. First introduced by astrophysicist Brandon Carter in 1973, the Anthropic Principle posits that the observed values of the fundamental constants and parameters of the universe must be compatible with the conditions necessary for the existence of observers such as ourselves.

In other words, the Anthropic Principle suggests that we observe a universe that appears to be finely-tuned for life because, in a universe that is not finely-tuned, observers like us could not exist to make observations. This idea has given rise to two primary formulations of the Anthropic Principle:

Weak Anthropic Principle (WAP): According to the WAP, our observations of the universe are necessarily constrained by the conditions required for our existence. This principle simply acknowledges that our observations of the universe are not random, but are instead biased by the fact that we exist.

Strong Anthropic Principle (SAP): The SAP goes a step further, positing that the universe must have properties that allow for the emergence of intelligent life. In other words, the SAP suggests that the existence of intelligent observers is not just a coincidence, but rather an inherent feature of the universe.

Fine-tuning: The Delicate Balance of the Cosmos

The concept of fine-tuning refers to the observation that the fundamental constants and parameters of the universe appear to be finely-tuned to allow for the formation of complex structures, such as galaxies, stars, and planets, as well as the emergence of life. This fine-tuning is evident in various aspects of the universe, including the values of the gravitational constant, the strong nuclear force, the weak nuclear force, and the cosmological constant, among others.

The apparent fine-tuning of the universe has led some scientists and philosophers to argue in favor of the existence of a multiverse, in which our universe is just one of an infinite number of parallel universes, each with its own unique set of physical laws and constants. In this framework, the fine-tuning of our universe can be explained as a natural consequence of the vast diversity of the multiverse, with life emerging in those universes that possess the necessary conditions for its existence.

Implications of the Anthropic Principle and Fine-tuning

The Anthropic Principle and the concept of fine-tuning have profound implications for our understanding of the universe and the nature of existence:

The Multiverse Hypothesis: The Anthropic Principle and the idea of fine-tuning lend support to the multiverse hypothesis, suggesting that our universe is just one of an infinite number of parallel universes with varying physical properties. In this context, the fine-tuning of our universe can be explained as a natural consequence of the vast diversity of the multiverse.

The Role of Chance and Necessity: The Anthropic Principle raises intriguing questions about the role of chance and necessity in the formation of the universe and the emergence of life. Are the observed properties of the universe a product of chance, or are they the result of some underlying principle or purpose?

The Limits of Scientific Explanation: The Anthropic Principle and the concept of fine-tuning highlight the limits of scientific explanation and invite us to consider the potential role of philosophical and metaphysical perspectives in our understanding of the cosmos. Can science alone provide a comprehensive account of the universe and its origins, or are there fundamental questions that remain beyond the reach of empirical investigation?

Implications for Human Civilization: The Anthropic Principle and fine-tuning have important implications for our understanding of human civilization and our place in the universe. If our existence is indeed a product of a delicate balance of cosmic forces, what does this mean for our future as a species, and how should we approach the challenges and opportunities that lie ahead?

The Anthropic Principle and the concept of fine-tuning offer fascinating insights into the nature of the universe and the potential existence of a vast, complex multiverse. By examining the delicate balance of the cosmos and the conditions necessary for the emergence of life, these ideas challenge our understanding of the universe's origins and its ultimate purpose, inviting us to consider the profound mysteries that lie at the heart of existence.

As we continue to explore the many fascinating aspects of quantum theory, the universe, and the multiverse, as well as their potential impact on human civilization and our understanding of the world around us, the Anthropic Principle and the idea of fine-tuning will remain central to theoretical investigations and philosophical debates. Through these inquiries, we aim to illuminate the enigmatic phenomena and infinite possibilities that shape the cosmos, inspiring a new generation of scientists, philosophers, and dreamers to ponder the vast expanse of the universe and the myriad wonders that await us in the uncharted territories of the multiverse.

In the chapters that follow, we will delve deeper into the realm of the quantum and grapple with the profound implications of the Anthropic Principle and fine-tuning, as well as their potential impact on human civilization and our understanding of the world around us. As we journey through the cosmos and explore the frontiers of human knowledge, we stand at the precipice of a new era of discovery and understanding, poised to unlock the secrets of the universe and redefine our place within the vast tapestry of existence.

CHAPTER 15: BRANE WORLDS AND EXTRA DIMENSIONS

Brane worlds and extra dimensions are fascinating concepts in the realm of theoretical physics, offering novel perspectives on the nature of the universe and the potential existence of parallel realities. In this chapter, we will explore the ideas of brane worlds and extra dimensions, examining their theoretical foundations, implications for our understanding of the cosmos, and the thought-provoking questions they raise about the fundamental nature of existence.

Brane Worlds: Parallel Universes on Membranes

In theoretical physics, brane worlds refer to the idea that our universe exists on a higher-dimensional membrane, or "brane," embedded within a larger, multi-dimensional space known as the "bulk." The concept of brane worlds arises from string theory and its extension, M-theory, which posit that the fundamental building blocks of the universe are not particles, but rather one-dimensional strings vibrating in multiple dimensions.

According to the brane world scenario, the familiar three dimensions of space and one dimension of time that we experience are confined to the brane, while additional dimensions are hidden within the bulk. The brane itself can be thought of as a four-dimensional slice of the higher-dimensional space, with other parallel branes potentially existing in close proximity to our own.

Extra Dimensions: Beyond the Familiar Four

The concept of extra dimensions is rooted in the idea that

the universe is not limited to the familiar four dimensions of space and time, but instead contains additional dimensions that are hidden from our direct observation. The idea of extra dimensions has a long history in theoretical physics, dating back to the work of the mathematician Theodor Kaluza and the physicist Oskar Klein in the early 20th century.

In the context of brane worlds and string theory, extra dimensions play a crucial role in unifying the various forces of nature and explaining the behavior of elementary particles. These additional dimensions are typically compactified, or "curled up," on scales too small for us to perceive directly. However, their existence has profound implications for our understanding of the universe and the fundamental laws that govern its behavior.

Implications of Brane Worlds and Extra Dimensions

The ideas of brane worlds and extra dimensions have far-reaching implications for our understanding of the universe and the nature of existence:

Unification of Forces: The existence of extra dimensions offers a potential path towards the unification of the fundamental forces of nature, such as electromagnetism, the weak nuclear force, the strong nuclear force, and gravity. By incorporating additional dimensions into our models of the universe, we may be able to develop a consistent theoretical framework that unifies these seemingly disparate forces into a single, coherent description of reality.

The Cosmological Constant Problem: Extra dimensions and brane worlds may provide a solution to the cosmological constant problem, which relates to the observed value of the vacuum energy in the universe. The existence of extra dimensions and their interaction with the brane could potentially explain the small but non-zero value of the cosmological constant, offering new insights into the nature of dark energy and its role in the expansion of the universe.

The Hierarchy Problem: The concept of extra dimensions may also shed light on the hierarchy problem, which concerns the large discrepancy between the strengths of gravity and the other fundamental forces. By allowing gravity to propagate through the bulk while the other forces remain confined to the brane, brane world scenarios can potentially explain the observed weakness of gravity compared to the other forces.

The Search for Parallel Universes: Brane worlds and extra dimensions open the door to the possibility of parallel universes existing in close proximity to our own. These parallel branes could harbor their own unique set of physical laws and constants, giving rise to a vast, diverse multiverse that contains an untold number of potential realities.

Testable Predictions: While the concepts of brane worlds and extra dimensions may seem purely speculative, they do offer testable predictions that can be explored through experimental research. For example, the existence of extra dimensions could potentially be detected through the observation of miniature black holes at particle colliders or deviations from the inverse square law of gravity at small distances.

Brane worlds and extra dimensions offer a tantalizing glimpse into the hidden depths of the universe, inviting us to consider the existence of parallel realities and the far-reaching implications of a multi-dimensional cosmos. As we continue to explore the many fascinating aspects of quantum theory, the universe, and the multiverse, as well as their potential impact on human civilization and our understanding of the world around us, the ideas of brane worlds and extra dimensions will remain central to theoretical investigations and philosophical debates.

In the chapters that follow, we will delve deeper into the realm of the quantum and grapple with the profound implications of brane worlds and extra dimensions, as well as their potential impact on human civilization and our understanding of the world around us. As we journey through the cosmos and explore the frontiers of human knowledge, we stand at the precipice of a new era of discovery and understanding, poised to unlock the secrets of the universe and redefine our place within the vast tapestry of existence.

From the unification of the fundamental forces of nature to the potential existence of parallel universes, the study of brane worlds and extra dimensions promises to remain a fertile ground for scientific inquiry and philosophical speculation, offering new perspectives on the fundamental questions that have captivated humanity for millennia. As we delve deeper into the realm of the quantum and confront the enigmatic phenomena that lie at the heart of the cosmos, we are reminded of the infinite possibilities that await us in the uncharted territories of the multiverse, inspiring us to reach for the stars and explore the unknown with curiosity, courage, and a sense of wonder.

PART IV: QUANTUM MECHANICS AND CONSCIOUSNESS

The Quantum Mind Hypothesis
Decoherence and the Measurement Problem
Free Will and Quantum Determinism
Quantum Biology and the Origins of Life
The Role of Consciousness in the Universe

CHAPTER 16: THE QUANTUM MIND HYPOTHESIS

The Quantum Mind Hypothesis is a fascinating and controversial topic at the intersection of quantum physics, neuroscience, and philosophy. It proposes that the principles of quantum mechanics play a crucial role in the workings of the human mind and consciousness. In this chapter, we will explore the Quantum Mind Hypothesis, examining its theoretical foundations, the arguments for and against its validity, and the thought-provoking questions it raises about the nature of consciousness and the fundamental nature of reality.

The Quantum Mind Hypothesis: A Brief Overview

The Quantum Mind Hypothesis posits that the processes underlying human consciousness and cognition are fundamentally quantum in nature, involving quantum superposition, entanglement, and wave function collapse. Advocates of the Quantum Mind Hypothesis argue that the classical physics-based models of the brain are insufficient to explain the complexity and richness of human consciousness, and that a quantum description is necessary to account for the full range of cognitive phenomena.

One of the most well-known proponents of the Quantum Mind Hypothesis is the British physicist Sir Roger Penrose, who, in collaboration with the American anesthesiologist Stuart Hameroff, developed the Orchestrated Objective Reduction (Orch-OR) model of consciousness. According to the Orch-OR model, quantum processes take place within microtubules, which are tiny protein structures found in the brain's neurons. Penrose and Hameroff argue that these quantum processes give rise to consciousness through a process known as objective reduction.

Arguments for the Quantum Mind Hypothesis

Proponents of the Quantum Mind Hypothesis offer several arguments in favor of their view, including:

The Hard Problem of Consciousness: The Quantum Mind Hypothesis is often presented as a potential solution to the so-called "hard problem" of consciousness, which refers to the difficulty of explaining how subjective experiences, or qualia, arise from physical processes in the brain. Quantum mechanics, with its inherent nonlocality and observer-dependence, may provide a framework for understanding the relationship between mind and matter that classical physics cannot.

The Role of Superposition and Entanglement: Quantum superposition and entanglement are key features of quantum mechanics that may play a role in cognitive processes, enabling the simultaneous representation of multiple possibilities and the rapid processing of information in the brain.

The Potential for Nonlocality: The nonlocal nature of quantum mechanics, as demonstrated by phenomena such as quantum entanglement, suggests that the human mind may possess a fundamentally nonlocal aspect, potentially accounting for features of consciousness that are difficult to explain within a classical framework.

Arguments against the Quantum Mind Hypothesis

Critics of the Quantum Mind Hypothesis raise several objections to the idea that quantum mechanics plays a significant role in the workings of the human mind:

The Warm, Wet, and Noisy Brain: One of the primary objections to the Quantum Mind Hypothesis is the argument that the warm, wet, and noisy environment of the human brain is unsuitable for maintaining the delicate quantum states necessary for quantum computation. Quantum coherence, which is essential for quantum processes, is typically observed in extremely cold and isolated environments, far removed from the conditions found in the brain.

The Lack of Empirical Evidence: Critics argue that there is a lack of empirical evidence supporting the Quantum Mind Hypothesis. While some experimental results have been suggested as evidence for quantum effects in the brain, these findings are often disputed and have not been conclusively demonstrated.

Alternative Explanations: Many researchers argue that classical physics-based models of the brain, such as neural networks and connectionist models, are sufficient to explain the complexity and richness of human consciousness, without the need to invoke quantum mechanics.

The Quantum Mind Hypothesis is a captivating and contentious topic that continues to spark lively debate among scientists, philosophers, and thinkers from various fields. As we probe deeper into the mysteries of human consciousness and the nature of reality, the question of whether the human mind operates on a quantum level remains an intriguing possibility.

The debate surrounding the Quantum Mind Hypothesis highlights the many challenges and unanswered questions that persist in our understanding of the human mind, consciousness, and the fundamental nature of reality. As we continue to explore these enigmatic phenomena, new insights and discoveries may help to illuminate the complex interplay between the quantum and classical realms, and the role that these interactions may play in shaping our perceptions, thoughts, and experiences.

In the chapters that follow, we will delve further into the realm of quantum theory, the universe, and the multiverse, as well as their potential impact on human civilization and our understanding of the world around us. As we journey through the cosmos and explore the frontiers of human knowledge, we stand at the precipice of a new era of discovery and understanding, poised to unlock the secrets of the universe and redefine our place within the vast tapestry of existence.

From the enigmatic nature of human consciousness to the uncharted territories of the quantum realm, the study of the Quantum Mind Hypothesis offers a fascinating glimpse into the unexplored frontiers of science, philosophy, and the human experience. As we confront the profound questions and paradoxes that lie at the heart of existence, we are reminded of the infinite possibilities that await us in the vast expanse of the universe and the myriad wonders that lie hidden within the depths of the human mind, inspiring us to reach for the stars and explore the unknown with curiosity, courage, and a sense of wonder.

CHAPTER 17: DECOHERENCE AND THE MEASUREMENT PROBLEM

One of the most puzzling and enduring issues in quantum mechanics is the measurement problem, which concerns the apparent conflict between the deterministic evolution of quantum systems described by the Schrödinger equation and the probabilistic nature of measurement outcomes. Decoherence is a concept that has emerged as a potential solution to this problem, offering a way to reconcile the seemingly paradoxical aspects of quantum mechanics. In this chapter, we will delve into the concept of decoherence and its implications for the measurement problem, examining the theoretical foundations, potential applications, and the thought-provoking questions it raises about the nature of reality.

Decoherence: A Brief Overview

Decoherence is a process by which a quantum system loses its quantum coherence, or its ability to exhibit quantum mechanical behavior, as a result of interactions with its environment. In essence, decoherence causes a quantum system to transition from a state of superposition, in which it simultaneously exists in multiple states, to a definite state upon measurement. Decoherence occurs due to the entanglement between the quantum system and its environment, which effectively destroys the fragile quantum coherence and leads to the emergence of classical-like behavior.

The Role of Decoherence in the Measurement Problem

The measurement problem in quantum mechanics arises from the apparent contradiction between the deterministic evolution of a quantum system, as described by the Schrödinger equation, and the probabilistic nature of measurement outcomes. According to the standard interpretation of quantum mechanics, known as the Copenhagen interpretation, a quantum system exists in a superposition of states until it is measured, at which point its wave function collapses to a single, definite state.

Decoherence offers a potential resolution to the measurement problem by explaining the apparent wave function collapse as a result of the quantum system's interaction with its environment. Rather than a true collapse of the wave function, decoherence suggests that the transition from a superposition to a definite state is an emergent phenomenon that arises from the entanglement between the quantum system and its environment.

Implications of Decoherence for Quantum Mechanics

The concept of decoherence has several important implications for our understanding of quantum mechanics and the nature of reality:

The Emergence of Classical Behavior: Decoherence provides a mechanism for the emergence of classical behavior from quantum systems, explaining how the seemingly paradoxical aspects of quantum mechanics can give rise to the familiar, deterministic world we experience at the macroscopic level.

The Interpretation of Quantum Mechanics: By offering a potential solution to the measurement problem, decoherence has significant implications for the interpretation of quantum mechanics. While it does not provide a complete resolution to the issue, decoherence informs ongoing debates about the nature of wave function collapse and the role of observers in the quantum world.

Quantum Computing and Information Theory: Decoherence is a central issue in the development of quantum computing and quantum information theory, as it represents a major obstacle to maintaining the fragile quantum states necessary for quantum computation. Understanding and mitigating decoherence is crucial for the advancement of quantum technologies and their potential applications.

Challenges and Open Questions

Despite its promise as a potential solution to the measurement problem, decoherence is not without its challenges and open questions:

The Nature of Wave Function Collapse: While decoherence provides a mechanism for the apparent collapse of the wave function, it does not fully explain the nature of the collapse or the emergence of definite outcomes from quantum superpositions.

The Role of Consciousness: Decoherence does not address the potential role of consciousness in the measurement process, a topic that remains a subject of ongoing debate and speculation.

The Ontological Status of the Wave Function: The concept of decoherence does not provide a definitive answer to the question of whether the wave function represents a physically real entity or merely a mathematical tool for predicting measurement outcomes. This question, known as the ontological status of the wave function, remains a subject of intense debate among physicists and philosophers.

Decoherence is a fascinating and important concept in the study of quantum mechanics, shedding light on the elusive measurement problem and the emergence of classical behavior from quantum systems. As we continue to explore the mysteries of the quantum realm, decoherence offers valuable insights into the complex interplay between quantum systems and their environments, as well as the potential role of observers in shaping the nature of reality.

In the chapters that follow, we will delve further into the realm of quantum theory, the universe, and the multiverse, as well as their potential impact on human civilization and our understanding of the world around us. As we journey through the cosmos and explore the frontiers of human knowledge, we stand at the precipice of a new era of discovery and understanding, poised to unlock the secrets of the universe and redefine our place within the vast tapestry of existence.

From the intricate dance of decoherence and entanglement to the enigmatic nature of wave function collapse, the study of quantum mechanics promises to remain a fertile ground for scientific inquiry and philosophical speculation, offering new perspectives on the fundamental questions that have captivated humanity for millennia. As we confront the profound challenges and paradoxes that lie at the heart of the quantum world, we are reminded of the infinite possibilities that await us in the uncharted territories of the cosmos, inspiring us to reach for the stars and explore the unknown with curiosity, courage, and a sense of wonder.

CHAPTER 18: FREE WILL AND QUANTUM DETERMINISM

The debate surrounding free will and determinism has been a topic of philosophical inquiry for centuries. With the advent of quantum mechanics, the discussion has taken on new dimensions, as the probabilistic nature of quantum mechanics appears to challenge the deterministic worldview that underlies classical physics. In this chapter, we will explore the implications of quantum mechanics for our understanding of free will and determinism, examining the philosophical and scientific arguments for and against the existence of free will within a quantum framework.

Free Will and Determinism: A Brief Overview

Free will is the ability to make choices that are not determined by external factors or internal constraints. Determinism, on the other hand, is the philosophical view that all events, including human thoughts and actions, are determined by prior causes. In a deterministic universe, the future is fully determined by the past, and there is no room for free will.

Quantum mechanics, with its inherent probabilistic nature, seems to offer a potential challenge to the deterministic worldview. According to quantum mechanics, the outcome of a measurement on a quantum system cannot be precisely predicted; instead, it is governed by a probability distribution. This apparent indeterminacy has led some to argue that quantum mechanics provides a foundation for free will, by allowing for the possibility of genuinely undetermined choices.

Quantum Determinism and the Role of Probability

While the probabilistic nature of quantum mechanics appears to challenge the notion of determinism, it is essential to recognize that quantum mechanics is not inherently indeterministic. Rather, quantum mechanics is governed by a form of determinism known as quantum determinism, which is distinct from classical determinism.

In quantum determinism, the evolution of a quantum system is described by the Schrödinger equation, which is a deterministic equation that governs the time-evolution of the system's wave function. The probabilistic aspect of quantum mechanics arises when a measurement is made on the system, at which point the wave function appears to collapse to a definite state, with the outcome determined by a probability distribution.

The relationship between quantum determinism and the probabilistic nature of measurement outcomes is a subject of ongoing debate among physicists and philosophers. Some argue that the apparent indeterminacy of quantum mechanics is an artifact of our incomplete understanding of the underlying reality, while others contend that the probabilistic nature of quantum mechanics reflects a fundamental aspect of the universe.

Implications of Quantum Mechanics for Free Will

The implications of quantum mechanics for the debate surrounding free will are complex and multifaceted. Some of the key arguments and perspectives include:

The Indeterminacy Argument: Some proponents of free will argue that the indeterminacy of quantum mechanics provides a basis for free will, as it allows for the possibility of genuinely undetermined choices. However, critics of this view contend that indeterminacy alone does not necessarily imply free will, as it may simply replace determinism with randomness.

The Quantum Mind Hypothesis: As discussed in Chapter 16,

the Quantum Mind Hypothesis posits that the principles of quantum mechanics play a crucial role in the workings of the human mind and consciousness. If this hypothesis is correct, it could have significant implications for the debate surrounding free will, as it suggests that our thoughts and choices may be influenced by inherently quantum processes.

Compatibilism and Incompatibilism: The debate surrounding free will and determinism is often framed in terms of compatibilism (the view that free will and determinism are compatible) and incompatibilism (the view that free will and determinism are incompatible). The implications of quantum mechanics for this debate are not clear-cut, as the probabilistic nature of quantum mechanics challenges classical determinism but does not necessarily provide a definitive answer to the question of free will.

The cosmos and probe the frontiers of human knowledge, we stand at the threshold of a new era of discovery and understanding, poised to unlock the secrets of the universe and redefine our place within the vast tapestry of existence.

From the intricate dance of quantum coherence in photosynthesis to the enigmatic role of quantum entanglement in biological systems, the study of quantum biology promises to revolutionize our understanding of life and its origins. As we confront the profound mysteries that lie at the heart of living systems, we are reminded of the infinite possibilities that await us in the uncharted territories of the cosmos, inspiring us to reach for the stars and explore the unknown with curiosity, courage, and a sense of wonder.

As we continue our journey through the chapters of this book, we will delve into even more fascinating aspects of quantum theory, the universe, and the multiverse. We will explore topics such as the potential role of quantum mechanics in the development of human civilization, the possibility of time travel and parallel universes, and the profound philosophical questions that arise from our exploration of the quantum realm.

Together, we will embark on an intellectual adventure that spans the depths of space and time, probing the boundaries of human knowledge and expanding our understanding of the universe and our place within it. As we delve deeper into the mysteries of quantum mechanics, we will uncover new perspectives on the nature of reality, challenging our assumptions about the world around us and revealing the breathtaking complexity and beauty of the cosmos.

CHAPTER 19: QUANTUM BIOLOGY AND THE ORIGINS OF LIFE

Quantum biology is an emerging interdisciplinary field that seeks to understand the role of quantum mechanics in biological processes. It aims to bridge the gap between the microscopic world of quantum phenomena and the macroscopic world of living organisms. In this chapter, we will explore the implications of quantum mechanics for our understanding of the origins of life and examine several key biological processes that may be influenced by quantum phenomena.

Quantum Effects in Photosynthesis
Photosynthesis is the process by which plants, algae, and certain bacteria convert sunlight into chemical energy, which is then stored in the form of glucose or other organic molecules. It has been discovered that quantum effects play a role in the efficiency of photosynthesis, particularly in the initial stage known as the light-harvesting stage.

During this stage, light-absorbing pigments called chlorophyll capture photons and transfer their energy to reaction centers, where the energy is used to drive chemical reactions. Research has shown that this energy transfer process is highly efficient, with almost no energy loss. One possible explanation for this efficiency is a quantum phenomenon known as quantum coherence, where the energy travels through multiple pathways simultaneously, allowing it to find the most efficient route to the reaction centers.

Quantum Tunneling in Enzymatic Reactions

Enzymes are biological catalysts that speed up chemical reactions in living organisms. They are essential for life, as they regulate the rates of metabolic processes and ensure that reactions occur at a sufficient speed to sustain life. Quantum tunneling, a phenomenon in which particles can pass through energy barriers that would be insurmountable according to classical physics, has been suggested to play a role in enzymatic reactions.

It has been proposed that quantum tunneling may allow protons, electrons, or other particles involved in enzymatic reactions to pass through energy barriers more easily, thus increasing the speed and efficiency of the reaction. This could help explain the remarkable catalytic power of enzymes, which often exceed the rates that would be predicted by classical models.

Quantum Entanglement and DNA

The structure and function of DNA, the molecule that carries genetic information in living organisms, have long fascinated scientists. Recent research has suggested that quantum entanglement, a phenomenon in which the properties of two or more particles become correlated even across large distances, may play a role in the stability of DNA.

Some studies have proposed that the hydrogen bonds that hold the two strands of the DNA double helix together may exhibit quantum entanglement, contributing to the stability and integrity of the DNA molecule. However, more research is needed to fully understand the implications of these findings and their potential significance for our understanding of genetics and molecular biology.

The Role of Quantum Mechanics in the Origins of Life

The origins of life remain one of the most intriguing and complex questions in science. Some researchers have proposed that quantum mechanics may have played a role in the formation of the first organic molecules and the development of life on Earth. For example, quantum tunneling may have facilitated the formation of chemical bonds between atoms and molecules in the primordial soup, potentially increasing the likelihood of the emergence of life.

Moreover, some researchers have suggested that the unique properties of quantum mechanics, such as superposition and entanglement, could have contributed to the development of the first self-replicating molecules, which would have been a crucial step in the emergence of life.

Quantum biology is a rapidly growing field that seeks to uncover the fascinating connections between the quantum world and the biological processes that underpin life. While our understanding of these connections is still in its infancy, the potential implications of quantum mechanics for our understanding of the origins of life and key biological processes are profound. As research in this area continues to advance, we may gain new insights into the fundamental nature of life itself and the role that quantum phenomena play in shaping the complex and intricate world of living organisms.

Quantum Effects in Sensory Perception

Sensory perception is another area where quantum mechanics may have a significant impact. One example is the sense of smell, or olfaction, which relies on the detection of specific molecules called odorants. It has been suggested that the interaction between odorant molecules and olfactory receptors in the nose may involve a quantum process known as electron tunneling. This theory, known as the "quantum nose" hypothesis, posits that the electron tunneling allows the receptors to detect subtle differences in molecular vibrations, enabling us to distinguish between a vast array of scents.

Another example is the process of vision. The detection of light by the photoreceptor cells in the retina, called rods and cones, relies on a process called photoisomerization, which involves the absorption of photons and the subsequent change in the conformation of a molecule called retinal. Some researchers have suggested that quantum coherence may play a role in the efficiency and sensitivity of this process, enabling the photoreceptor cells to detect single photons of light.

Quantum Mechanics and the Evolution of Life
The role of quantum mechanics in the evolution of life is another intriguing area of research. It has been proposed that the unique properties of quantum systems, such as the ability to explore multiple states simultaneously through quantum superposition, could have influenced the course of evolution by facilitating the exploration of a broader range of genetic variations and phenotypes.

For example, some researchers have suggested that quantum effects could play a role in genetic mutations, which are a driving force of evolution. Quantum tunneling or other quantum phenomena might increase the rate at which genetic mutations occur, potentially enabling organisms to adapt more rapidly to changing environmental conditions.

The Future of Quantum Biology
As our understanding of quantum biology continues to grow, it is likely that we will uncover even more ways in which quantum phenomena influence the processes of life. These discoveries could have far-reaching implications for our understanding of biology, evolution, and the origins of life. Moreover, the insights gained from studying quantum biology may also have practical

applications, such as the development of new drugs and therapies, more efficient energy production methods, and advanced materials inspired by nature.

In conclusion, the field of quantum biology is a testament to the remarkable interconnectedness of the natural world, revealing that even the seemingly separate realms of quantum mechanics and biology are intimately linked. As we continue to explore this fascinating frontier, we may discover that the quantum realm is not just the domain of the very small, but a fundamental aspect of the living world that surrounds us.

CHAPTER 20: THE ROLE OF CONSCIOUSNESS IN THE UNIVERSE

Consciousness has long been a subject of fascination and debate for philosophers, scientists, and theologians alike. It is a central aspect of the human experience, yet its nature, origins, and role in the universe remain elusive and enigmatic. With the advent of quantum mechanics, the question of consciousness has taken on new dimensions, as the potential interplay between consciousness and the quantum realm opens up new avenues for exploration and inquiry. In this chapter, we will delve into the role of consciousness in the universe, examining its relationship with quantum mechanics and its implications for our understanding of reality.

The Nature of Consciousness

Consciousness is often described as the subjective experience of being aware of oneself and one's environment. It encompasses a wide range of mental phenomena, including perception, thought, emotion, and self-awareness. Despite its centrality to the human experience, the nature of consciousness remains one of the most significant unresolved questions in science and philosophy.

Various theories have been proposed to explain the nature of consciousness, ranging from materialistic approaches that seek to reduce consciousness to physical processes in the brain, to dualistic perspectives that posit the existence of a non-material mind distinct from the body. The relationship between consciousness and the physical world remains a topic of intense debate and investigation, with no consensus yet reached on the fundamental nature of conscious experience.

Consciousness and Quantum Mechanics

The advent of quantum mechanics has introduced new and intriguing possibilities for the study of consciousness. Some of the key areas of inquiry at the intersection of consciousness and quantum mechanics include:

The Observer Effect and the Role of Consciousness in Measurement: As discussed in Chapter 5, the act of observation plays a central role in the interpretation of quantum mechanics, with the wave function of a quantum system appearing to collapse to a definite state upon measurement. This apparent dependence of quantum phenomena on observation has led some to propose that consciousness may play a fundamental role in shaping the nature of reality, either by directly causing the collapse of the wave function or by somehow selecting among the various possible outcomes of a measurement.

The Quantum Mind Hypothesis: As explored in Chapter 16, the Quantum Mind Hypothesis posits that the principles of quantum mechanics may play a crucial role in the workings of the human mind and consciousness. If this hypothesis is correct, it could have profound implications for our understanding of the relationship between consciousness and the physical world, suggesting that our thoughts and experiences may be deeply intertwined with the fabric of the universe.

Quantum Nonlocality and the Unity of Consciousness: Quantum nonlocality, as described in Chapter 4, is a phenomenon in which the properties of two or more particles become correlated in such a way that the state of one particle cannot be described independently of the state of the others, regardless of the distance between them. Some have speculated that this principle of nonlocality may have implications for our understanding of consciousness, potentially providing a basis for the apparent unity of conscious experience.

The Role of Consciousness in the Universe

The potential relationship between consciousness and quantum mechanics raises intriguing questions about the role of consciousness in the universe. Some of the key perspectives and hypotheses include:

Consciousness as a Fundamental Aspect of Reality: Some researchers and philosophers argue that consciousness may be a fundamental aspect of reality, on par with space, time, and matter. This view, often referred to as panpsychism or cosmopsychism, posits that consciousness is an inherent property of the universe, with all matter possessing some form of conscious experience.

The Participatory Universe Hypothesis: Astrophysicist John Archibald Wheeler proposed the idea of a "participatory universe," in which conscious observers play a critical role in shaping the nature of reality itself. According to this hypothesis, the universe and consciousness are fundamentally interconnected, with the act of observation actively participating in the creation and evolution of the cosmos.

The Integrated Information Theory (IIT): Developed by neuroscientist Giulio Tononi, the Integrated Information Theory is a mathematical framework that attempts to quantify the degree of consciousness present in any given physical system. According to IIT, consciousness arises from the integration of information within a system, with the level of consciousness proportional to the amount of integrated information. This theory suggests that consciousness may be a universal property of complex, highly integrated systems, whether biological or non-biological.

The Orchestrated Objective Reduction (Orch-OR) Theory:

Proposed by physicist Roger Penrose and anesthesiologist Stuart Hameroff, the Orch-OR theory postulates that consciousness arises from quantum computations occurring within microtubules – tiny, tube-like structures found in the cytoskeleton of neurons. According to this theory, conscious experience results from the orchestrated collapse of quantum superpositions within these microtubules, with the brain acting as a quantum computer.

Implications and Future Directions

The exploration of consciousness and its relationship with the universe holds profound implications for our understanding of reality, the nature of existence, and our place within the cosmos. As we continue to investigate the mysteries of consciousness and the potential interplay between conscious experience and the quantum realm, we may uncover new insights into the nature of reality and the origins of our own self-awareness.

Future research in this area is likely to encompass a wide range of disciplines, from neuroscience and psychology to physics and philosophy, as scientists and thinkers from diverse backgrounds collaborate to unravel the enigma of consciousness. As our knowledge of the universe expands, and our understanding of the role of consciousness within it deepens, we stand at the cusp of a new era of discovery – one that promises to challenge our most fundamental assumptions about the nature of reality and the limits of human understanding.

In the chapters to come, we will continue to explore the vast and fascinating landscape of quantum theory, the universe, and the multiverse, examining their implications for human civilization and the future of our species. From the development of advanced technologies to the search for extraterrestrial life, the unfolding story of quantum mechanics and its relationship with the cosmos holds the potential to reshape our understanding of the universe and our place within it, opening up new horizons of discovery and wonder.

PART V: THE IMPACT OF QUANTUM THEORY ON HUMAN CIVILIZATION

Quantum Computing: The Next Frontier
Nanotechnology and Quantum Materials
Quantum Communication and Cryptography
The Role of Quantum Mechanics in Artificial Intelligence
The Future of Energy Production: Quantum Fusion

CHAPTER 21: QUANTUM COMPUTING: THE NEXT FRONTIER

Quantum computing represents a revolutionary leap in the field of computing and information processing. Harnessing the principles of quantum mechanics, quantum computers have the potential to solve problems that are currently intractable for classical computers, transforming industries and paving the way for groundbreaking scientific discoveries. In this chapter, we will explore the foundations of quantum computing, the current state of the field, and the potential impact of this transformative technology on human civilization and our understanding of the universe.

The Basics of Quantum Computing

Quantum computing relies on the principles of quantum mechanics to process information in a fundamentally different way than classical computers. While classical computers use bits to represent information as binary values (0 or 1), quantum computers utilize qubits, which can exist in a superposition of both 0 and 1 simultaneously, thanks to the principle of quantum superposition.

This unique property of qubits allows quantum computers to perform many calculations in parallel, providing an exponential speedup in processing power for certain types of problems. Furthermore, the principle of quantum entanglement enables qubits to become correlated in such a way that the state of one qubit cannot be described independently of the state of the others, allowing for more efficient information processing and communication.

Current State of Quantum Computing

Quantum computing is still in its early stages of development, with researchers around the world working to build and refine the technology. Some of the key milestones and challenges in the field include:

Quantum Supremacy: In 2019, Google announced that its quantum computer, Sycamore, had achieved "quantum supremacy," meaning it had performed a calculation that would be practically impossible for a classical computer to complete within a reasonable timeframe. This milestone marked a significant step forward in the development of quantum computing, demonstrating the potential of this technology to tackle problems beyond the reach of classical computers.

Error Correction and Fault Tolerance: One of the major challenges in building practical quantum computers is addressing the issue of error correction and fault tolerance. Quantum systems are highly susceptible to noise and decoherence, which can lead to errors in computation. Developing effective error-correcting codes and fault-tolerant architectures is crucial for the successful implementation of large-scale quantum computers.

Quantum Algorithms: The development of efficient quantum algorithms is essential for unlocking the full potential of quantum computing. While some algorithms, such as Shor's algorithm for integer factorization and Grover's algorithm for unstructured search, have demonstrated the potential for exponential speedup over classical algorithms, further research is needed to develop new quantum algorithms and identify their practical applications.

The Impact of Quantum Computing

Quantum computing holds the potential to revolutionize a wide range of industries and applications, including cryptography, optimization, materials science, and artificial intelligence. Some of the key implications and potential impacts of this technology include:

Cryptography and Cybersecurity: Quantum computing poses a significant threat to current cryptographic systems, as algorithms like Shor's can efficiently factor large prime numbers, breaking the security of widely used encryption methods such as RSA. On the other hand, quantum computers also offer the potential for new, more secure encryption techniques, such as quantum key distribution.

Drug Discovery and Materials Science: Quantum computers have the potential to simulate complex quantum systems, such as molecules and materials, with unprecedented accuracy. This capability could revolutionize drug discovery and materials science, enabling the development of new drugs, materials, and industrial processes with enhanced properties and performance.

Optimization and Machine Learning: Quantum computing offers new approaches to solving complex optimization problems, which have widespread applications in logistics, finance, and machine learning. By harnessing the power of quantum algorithms, researchers hope to develop more efficient optimization techniques and advance the field of artificial intelligence.

Quantum computing represents a bold new frontier in the realm of computing and information processing, with the potential to reshape industries, drive scientific breakthroughs, and transform our understanding of the universe. As researchers continue to advance the field and overcome the challenges associated with building practical quantum computers, the implications of this technology are likely to be far-reaching and profound.

In the coming years, quantum computing may revolutionize fields such as cryptography, drug discovery, materials science, and artificial intelligence, opening up new possibilities for innovation and discovery. Furthermore, the development of quantum computing may shed light on the fundamental nature of reality and the role of consciousness in the universe, as explored in previous chapters.

As we continue to delve into the fascinating world of quantum theory, the universe, and the multiverse, we will examine the potential impact of these emerging technologies on human civilization and the future of our species. From the search for extraterrestrial life to the exploration of the deepest mysteries of space and time, the unfolding story of quantum mechanics and its relationship with the cosmos holds the promise of unlocking new horizons of knowledge and understanding, forever changing our perspective on the universe and our place within it.

In the following chapters, we will further explore the myriad ways in which quantum theory intersects with and influences various aspects of our lives, our civilization, and our understanding of the cosmos. Through this journey, we hope to provide a comprehensive and engaging exploration of the vast and complex tapestry of quantum mechanics, the universe, and the multiverse, inspiring readers to reflect on the profound implications of these concepts and to continue the pursuit of knowledge and discovery.

CHAPTER 22: NANOTECHNOLOGY AND QUANTUM MATERIALS

Nanotechnology is the manipulation and control of matter at the atomic and molecular scale, typically within the range of 1 to 100 nanometers. This emerging field has the potential to revolutionize various industries and scientific disciplines, as it allows for the creation of new materials and devices with unique properties and functions. Quantum materials, in particular, are a class of materials whose properties and behavior are governed by the principles of quantum mechanics. In this chapter, we will explore the foundations of nanotechnology and quantum materials, their potential applications, and the ways in which they may reshape our understanding of the universe and impact human civilization.

Nanotechnology: The Basics

Nanotechnology is an interdisciplinary field that encompasses various scientific disciplines, including physics, chemistry, materials science, and engineering. At the nanoscale, the properties of materials can differ significantly from their bulk counterparts, exhibiting unique electrical, optical, and mechanical properties. This is due to the increased importance of quantum effects and surface-to-volume ratios at the nanoscale.

Some of the key techniques and tools used in nanotechnology include:

Scanning Probe Microscopy: Techniques such as atomic force microscopy (AFM) and scanning tunneling microscopy (STM) enable researchers to image and manipulate individual atoms and molecules, providing valuable insights into the properties and behavior of materials at the nanoscale.

Self-Assembly: Self-assembly is a process by which molecules and nanoparticles spontaneously organize themselves into complex structures through non-covalent interactions. This bottom-up approach to nanofabrication allows for the creation of intricate nanostructures with minimal external intervention.

Top-Down Fabrication: Top-down approaches, such as lithography and etching, involve the patterning and removal of material to create nanostructures. These techniques have been widely used in the semiconductor industry and are being adapted for the fabrication of novel nanoscale devices and materials.

Quantum Materials

Quantum materials are a class of materials whose properties and behavior are determined by quantum mechanical effects, such as superconductivity, topological states, and quantum confinement. These materials hold great promise for a wide range of applications, from electronics and energy storage to quantum computing and sensing. Some examples of quantum materials include:

Graphene: A single layer of carbon atoms arranged in a hexagonal lattice, graphene is an extraordinary material with exceptional electronic, thermal, and mechanical properties. Its unique electronic structure and high carrier mobility make it an ideal candidate for high-performance electronic devices and sensors.

Topological Insulators: These materials exhibit a unique electronic behavior in which the bulk of the material is insulating, but the surface conducts electricity. Top ological insulators hold promise for applications in spintronics and quantum computing, as they can support the existence of exotic quasiparticles, such as Majorana fermions, which could be used as the building blocks for topological quantum computers.

High-Temperature Superconductors: Superconductivity is a phenomenon in which a material's electrical resistance drops to zero below a certain critical temperature, allowing for the lossless transmission of electrical current. High-temperature superconductors can exhibit this behavior at relatively higher temperatures, making them more practical for real-world applications, such as energy transmission, magnetic levitation, and advanced medical imaging devices.

Applications and Impacts

Nanotechnology and quantum materials have the potential to revolutionize a wide range of industries and scientific disciplines, with far-reaching implications for human civilization and our understanding of the universe. Some of the key applications and impacts of these technologies include:

Electronics and Computing: Nanotechnology and quantum materials offer new approaches to designing faster, more energy-efficient electronic devices, including transistors, memory devices, and quantum computers. These advances could lead to the development of more powerful computers, enabling us to tackle complex problems and simulations that are currently intractable for classical computers.

Energy Storage and Conversion: Nanomaterials and quantum materials can enhance the performance of batteries, solar cells, and fuel cells, enabling more efficient energy storage and conversion. These advances could pave the way for cleaner, more sustainable energy sources and help address the global energy crisis.

Medicine and Healthcare: Nanotechnology offers a wide range of applications in medicine and healthcare, including targeted drug delivery, advanced diagnostics, and regenerative medicine.

Quantum materials, such as graphene, also have potential applications in biosensing and medical imaging, leading to more accurate and less invasive diagnostic tools.

Environmental Remediation: Nanotechnology and quantum materials can be used to develop more effective methods for environmental remediation, such as the removal of pollutants and contaminants from water and air. This could help address pressing global challenges, such as pollution and climate change.

Nanotechnology and quantum materials represent a new frontier in materials science, with the potential to transform industries, drive scientific breakthroughs, and reshape our understanding of the universe. As we continue to explore the fascinating world of quantum theory, the universe, and the multiverse, the development and application of these advanced materials may unlock new insights into the nature of reality and our place within the cosmos.

In the coming chapters, we will further examine the ways in which quantum theory intersects with and influences various aspects of our lives, our civilization, and our understanding of the universe. Through this journey, we aim to provide an engaging and comprehensive exploration of the vast and complex tapestry of quantum mechanics, the universe, and the multiverse, inspiring readers to reflect on the profound implications of these concepts and to continue the pursuit of knowledge and discovery.

CHAPTER 23: QUANTUM COMMUNICATION AND CRYPTOGRAPHY

Quantum communication and cryptography are branches of quantum information science that exploit the principles of quantum mechanics to enable secure transmission and processing of information. These technologies hold great promise for enhancing cybersecurity, providing new methods for secure communication, and addressing potential threats posed by quantum computing to existing encryption schemes. In this chapter, we will explore the foundations of quantum communication and cryptography, their potential applications, and the ways in which they may impact human civilization and our understanding of the universe.

Quantum Communication

Quantum communication involves the transmission of information encoded in quantum states, such as the polarization states of photons or the spin states of electrons. By harnessing the unique properties of quantum mechanics, such as superposition and entanglement, quantum communication offers significant advantages over classical communication methods, including enhanced security, reduced noise, and potentially faster information transmission.

Some of the key concepts and techniques in quantum communication include:

Quantum Key Distribution (QKD): QKD is a method for generating and securely distributing encryption keys between two parties using the principles of quantum mechanics. By encoding key information in quantum states, QKD protocols can guarantee the security of the key distribution process, as any attempt to intercept or tamper with the key will introduce detectable disturbances due to the observer effect.

Quantum Repeaters: Quantum repeaters are devices that can extend the range of quantum communication by entangling and transmitting quantum states over long distances. These devices are essential for overcoming the attenuation and decoherence that occur during the transmission of quantum states through optical fibers or free space.

Quantum Networks: Quantum networks are an emerging concept that envisions a global infrastructure for quantum communication, connecting quantum devices and users around the world. By leveraging the principles of quantum mechanics, quantum networks have the potential to enable secure, efficient, and novel forms of communication and information processing.

Quantum Cryptography

Quantum cryptography is the application of quantum mechanics to the field of cryptography, offering new methods for securing communication and protecting sensitive information from unauthorized access. Quantum cryptography can provide provable security based on the fundamental laws of physics, rather than relying on the computational complexity of cryptographic algorithms, as in classical cryptography.

Some of the key concepts and techniques in quantum cryptography include:

Quantum Key Distribution (QKD): As mentioned earlier, QKD is a central concept in quantum cryptography, enabling the secure generation and distribution of encryption keys between two parties. Protocols such as BB84 and E91 have demonstrated the feasibility of QKD in practical settings, with commercial QKD systems already available on the market.

Post-Quantum Cryptography: Post-quantum cryptography refers to cryptographic algorithms that are resistant to attacks by quantum computers. These algorithms are designed to protect sensitive information from potential threats posed by the advent of large-scale quantum computers, which could break widely used encryption schemes, such as RSA and elliptic curve cryptography.

Quantum Digital Signatures: Quantum digital signatures are a method for ensuring the integrity and authenticity of transmitted information using quantum states. Like classical digital signatures, quantum digital signatures can be used to verify the origin and contents of a message, but they offer enhanced security due to the unique properties of quantum mechanics.

Applications and Impacts

Quantum communication and cryptography have the potential to revolutionize the field of cybersecurity, with far-reaching implications for human civilization and our understanding of the universe. Some of the key applications and impacts of these technologies include:

Secure Communication: Quantum communication and cryptography offer new methods for securing communication between individuals, organizations, and governments, providing enhanced protection against eavesdropping, interception, and tampering.

Quantum Internet: The development of quantum networks and the quantum internet could enable novel forms of communication and information processing, such as quantum teleportation, distributed quantum computing, and secure multiparty computation. These advances could lead to a new era of communication, with far-reaching implications for science, technology, and society.

National Security and Defense: Quantum communication and cryptography could play a critical role in national security and defense by providing secure communication channels for military, intelligence, and diplomatic purposes. This could help protect sensitive information and infrastructure from cyberattacks and espionage, as well as maintain the strategic balance between nations.

Protection of Privacy and Personal Data: As our society becomes increasingly digital and interconnected, the protection of privacy and personal data is of paramount importance. Quantum communication and cryptography could provide enhanced security for personal communications, financial transactions, and other sensitive data, helping to safeguard individual privacy and prevent identity theft and fraud.

Safeguarding the Digital Economy: The digital economy relies on secure communication and data protection to function effectively. By ensuring the security of online transactions and protecting sensitive information from cyber threats, quantum communication and cryptography could help maintain the integrity and stability of the digital economy, fostering innovation and growth.

Quantum communication and cryptography represent a new frontier in information security, with the potential to transform the way we transmit, process, and protect information. As we continue to explore the fascinating world of quantum theory, the universe, and the multiverse, the development and application of these advanced technologies may unlock new insights into the nature of reality and our place within the cosmos.

In the coming chapters, we will further examine the ways in which quantum theory intersects with and influences various aspects of our lives, our civilization, and our understanding of the universe. Through this journey, we aim to provide an engaging and comprehensive exploration of the vast and complex tapestry of quantum mechanics, the universe, and the multiverse, inspiring readers to reflect on the profound implications of these concepts and to continue the pursuit of knowledge and discovery.

CHAPTER 24: THE ROLE OF QUANTUM MECHANICS IN ARTIFICIAL INTELLIGENCE

Artificial intelligence (AI) is an interdisciplinary field that seeks to develop intelligent machines capable of performing tasks that typically require human intelligence, such as problem-solving, learning, and decision-making. With the rapid advances in AI over the past few decades, researchers have begun exploring the potential applications of quantum mechanics in AI, seeking to harness the unique properties of quantum systems to enhance the capabilities of AI algorithms and systems. In this chapter, we will delve into the foundations of quantum AI, its potential applications, and the ways in which it may impact human civilization and our understanding of the universe.

Quantum Artificial Intelligence

Quantum artificial intelligence (QAI) is a branch of AI that leverages the principles of quantum mechanics to develop novel algorithms, models, and systems for information processing and decision-making. By exploiting the unique properties of quantum systems, such as superposition, entanglement, and quantum parallelism, QAI has the potential to significantly enhance the capabilities of AI, enabling more efficient and powerful algorithms for a wide range of tasks.

Some of the key concepts and techniques in QAI include:

Quantum Machine Learning (QML): Quantum machine learning is an emerging field that seeks to develop quantum algorithms and models for learning and inference. By harnessing the computational power of quantum computers, QML algorithms have the potential to significantly speed up the training and evaluation of machine learning models, enabling the analysis of larger datasets and the discovery of more complex patterns and relationships.

Quantum Optimization: Quantum optimization involves the development of quantum algorithms for solving complex optimization problems, which are ubiquitous in AI and many scientific disciplines. Quantum optimization algorithms, such as quantum annealing and the quantum approximate optimization algorithm (QAOA), have demonstrated the potential to outperform classical algorithms for certain problem instances, offering new approaches to tackling challenging optimization tasks.

Quantum Neural Networks (QNNs): Quantum neural networks are a class of quantum machine learning models that seek to generalize the concepts and techniques of classical neural networks to the quantum domain. QNNs have the potential to harness the unique properties of quantum systems, such as superposition and entanglement, to enable more efficient and powerful representations of information and learning dynamics.

Applications and Impacts

Quantum AI has the potential to revolutionize the field of artificial intelligence, with far-reaching implications for human civilization and our understanding of the universe. Some of the key applications and impacts of QAI include:

Enhanced AI Capabilities: By leveraging the principles of quantum mechanics, QAI could significantly enhance the capabilities of AI algorithms and systems, enabling more efficient and powerful solutions for a wide range of tasks, such as pattern recognition, prediction, and decision-making.

Drug Discovery and Materials Science: Quantum AI has the potential to accelerate the discovery of new drugs and materials by enabling more efficient exploration of the vast chemical and materials space. Quantum machine learning algorithms could help identify promising candidates for drug development and materials design, speeding up the research and development process and potentially leading to breakthroughs in medicine and technology.

Climate Modeling and Environmental Monitoring: Quantum AI could play a crucial role in climate modeling and environmental monitoring by enabling more accurate and efficient simulations of complex Earth systems. Quantum algorithms could help improve the precision and reliability of climate models, leading to a better understanding of the impacts of climate change and informing mitigation and adaptation strategies.

Finance and Economics: Quantum AI could have significant implications for the fields of finance and economics, enabling more efficient risk assessment, portfolio optimization, and financial modeling. Quantum algorithms could help identify new investment opportunities and better manage risk, potentially leading to increased stability and growth in financial markets.

Quantum artificial intelligence represents a new frontier in AI research, with the potential to transform the way we process and understand information, make decisions, and interact with the world. As we continue to explore the fascinating world of quantum mechanics, the universe, and the multiverse, the development and application of quantum AI technologies may unlock new insights into the nature of reality and our place within the cosmos.

In the coming chapters, we will further examine the ways in which quantum theory intersects with and influences various aspects of our lives, our civilization, and our understanding of the universe. Through this journey, we aim to provide an engaging and comprehensive exploration of the vast and complex tapestry of quantum mechanics, the universe, and the multiverse, inspiring readers to reflect on the profound implications of these concepts and to continue the pursuit of knowledge and discovery.

In the next chapter, we will delve into the intersection of quantum mechanics and human civilization, exploring the ways in which quantum theory has shaped and influenced the development of human societies, cultures, and technologies throughout history. This exploration will provide a unique perspective on the role of quantum mechanics in human civilization, highlighting the profound and lasting impact of these ideas on our world and our understanding of the universe.

CHAPTER 25: THE FUTURE OF ENERGY PRODUCTION: QUANTUM FUSION

As our understanding of quantum mechanics continues to deepen, its potential applications in various aspects of human civilization are increasingly being explored. One of the most promising and exciting areas where quantum mechanics could have a transformative impact is energy production, particularly in the field of nuclear fusion. In this chapter, we will discuss the concept of quantum fusion, its potential as a clean and virtually limitless source of energy, and how it could revolutionize the way we power our world.

Quantum Fusion: A New Frontier in Energy Production

Nuclear fusion is the process by which atomic nuclei combine to form heavier nuclei, releasing a tremendous amount of energy in the process. Fusion is the same process that powers the sun, where hydrogen nuclei fuse to form helium, releasing vast amounts of energy in the form of light and heat. Harnessing the power of nuclear fusion on Earth could provide a virtually limitless source of clean, sustainable energy, with minimal environmental impact and no long-lived radioactive waste.

Quantum fusion refers to the application of quantum mechanics principles and techniques in the pursuit of controlled nuclear fusion. By leveraging the unique properties of quantum systems, such as superposition, entanglement, and tunneling, researchers are developing novel approaches to achieving the conditions necessary for nuclear fusion, with the aim of making fusion energy a practical and viable solution to our growing energy needs.

Key Concepts and Techniques in Quantum Fusion

Quantum Tunneling: Quantum tunneling is a phenomenon in which particles can pass through energy barriers that would be insurmountable in classical mechanics. This effect is crucial for nuclear fusion, as it allows atomic nuclei to overcome the electrostatic repulsion between their positively charged protons and come close enough for the strong nuclear force to take effect, facilitating fusion.

Quantum Simulation: Quantum simulation is the use of quantum systems, such as quantum computers, to simulate and model the behavior of other quantum systems. In the context of quantum fusion, quantum simulation could help researchers understand the complex interactions between particles in a fusion plasma, potentially leading to more efficient and controlled fusion reactions.

Quantum Control: Quantum control involves the precise manipulation of quantum systems to achieve specific outcomes, such as optimizing the performance of a quantum computer or steering the course of a chemical reaction. In quantum fusion, quantum control could be used to manipulate the conditions within a fusion reactor, fine-tuning the plasma environment to maximize the probability of successful fusion events.

The Potential Impact of Quantum Fusion

The successful development of quantum fusion technology could have far-reaching implications for human civilization and our understanding of the universe, including:

Clean and Sustainable Energy: Quantum fusion could provide a virtually limitless source of clean, sustainable energy, with minimal environmental impact and no long-lived radioactive waste. This could help address the growing energy needs of our global population while mitigating the negative effects of climate change and reducing our reliance on fossil fuels.

Economic Growth: The widespread adoption of quantum fusion technology could drive significant economic growth, as the availability of abundant, low-cost energy would enable new industries, create jobs, and improve living standards around the world.

Space Exploration: Quantum fusion could revolutionize space exploration by providing an efficient and compact energy source for spacecraft propulsion. This could enable faster and more ambitious space missions, paving the way for human exploration of the solar system and beyond.

Geopolitical Stability: By providing a virtually limitless and universally accessible energy source, quantum fusion could help reduce global competition for limited fossil fuel resources, potentially fostering greater cooperation and stability among nations.

Quantum fusion represents a promising and transformative frontier in energy production, with the potential to revolutionize the way we power our world and shape the future of human civilization. As we continue to explore the fascinating world of quantum mechanics, the universe, and the multiverse, the development and application of quantum fusion technologies may unlock new insights into the nature of reality and our place within the cosmos.

In the coming chapters, we will further examine the ways in which quantum theory intersects with and influences various aspects of our lives, our civilization, and our understanding of the universe. Through this journey, we aim to provide an engaging and comprehensive exploration of the vast and complex tapestry of quantum mechanics, the universe, and the multiverse, inspiring readers to reflect on the profound implications of these concepts and to continue the pursuit of knowledge and discovery.

In the next chapter, we will explore the potential implications of quantum mechanics for the future of transportation and communication, delving into concepts such as quantum teleportation and quantum communication networks. This investigation will provide a glimpse into the fascinating possibilities that quantum mechanics may hold for the future of human civilization, offering a unique perspective on the role of these ideas in shaping our world and our understanding of the universe.

PART VI: QUANTUM EXPERIMENTS AND DISCOVERIES

The Double-Slit Experiment
The EPR Paradox and Bell's Theorem
Quantum Teleportation and its Applications
Quantum Superposition and Schrödinger's Cat
Recent Advances in Quantum Experiments

CHAPTER 26: THE DOUBLE-SLIT EXPERIMENT

The double-slit experiment is one of the most famous and intriguing experiments in the realm of quantum mechanics, as it demonstrates the wave-particle duality of matter and light in a visually striking manner. This groundbreaking experiment has not only deepened our understanding of quantum theory but has also played a pivotal role in shaping our perception of reality. In this chapter, we will delve into the history and details of the double-slit experiment, its implications for quantum mechanics, and the profound questions it raises about the nature of the universe.

The Double-Slit Experiment: A Quantum Mystery

The double-slit experiment was first performed by the English scientist Thomas Young in the early 19th century to demonstrate the wave-like behavior of light. In its original form, the experiment involved shining a beam of light through a pair of closely spaced slits in an opaque barrier. When the light passed through the slits, it created an interference pattern on a screen placed behind the barrier, with alternating bands of light and dark areas. This pattern was reminiscent of the interference patterns created by water waves passing through two openings, providing evidence that light behaves like a wave.

In the 20th century, with the development of quantum mechanics, scientists began to explore the behavior of particles such as electrons in the double-slit experiment. Surprisingly, it was discovered that when individual particles were sent through the double-slit apparatus one at a time, they also produced an interference pattern on the screen, as if they were behaving like waves. This astonishing result demonstrated the wave-particle duality of matter, a fundamental concept in quantum mechanics, which posits that particles can exhibit both wave-like and particle-like properties depending on the experimental context.

Key Concepts and Implications

Wave-Particle Duality: The double-slit experiment provides compelling evidence for the wave-particle duality of matter and light, a cornerstone of quantum mechanics. This duality suggests that the classical distinctions between waves and particles break down at the quantum level, and that the true nature of reality is more complex and counterintuitive than our everyday experiences might suggest.

The Observer Effect: Another intriguing aspect of the double-slit experiment is the role of observation in determining the outcome of the experiment. When a detector is placed near the slits to determine which slit the particle passes through, the interference pattern on the screen disappears, and the particles behave as if they were simply passing through one slit or the other. This phenomenon, known as the observer effect, suggests that the act of measurement can fundamentally alter the behavior of quantum systems.

The Nature of Reality: The double-slit experiment raises profound questions about the nature of reality and our role as observers in shaping the outcome of quantum events. The seemingly paradoxical behavior of particles in the double-slit experiment challenges our classical intuitions about the nature of the universe and invites us to explore the deeper implications of quantum mechanics for our understanding of reality.

The double-slit experiment is a powerful and captivating demonstration of the enigmatic properties of quantum mechanics, providing invaluable insights into the wave-particle duality of matter and light, the role of observation in quantum systems, and the fundamental nature of reality. As we continue our journey through the fascinating world of quantum mechanics, the universe, and the multiverse, the double-slit experiment serves as a compelling reminder of the rich tapestry of mysteries and wonders that await our exploration and understanding.

In the upcoming chapters, we will further investigate the ways in which quantum theory intersects with various aspects of human civilization, from the development of cutting-edge technologies to the philosophical and cultural implications of quantum mechanics. Through this exploration, we aim to provide an engaging and comprehensive account of the extraordinary world of quantum mechanics, the universe, and the multiverse, inspiring readers to contemplate the profound implications of these concepts and to continue the pursuit of knowledge and discovery.

In the next chapter, we will delve into the potential applications of quantum mechanics in the realm of medicine and healthcare, examining how the unique properties of quantum systems might be harnessed to develop novel therapies, diagnostics, and medical technologies. This investigation will provide a glimpse into the fascinating possibilities that quantum mechanics may hold for the future of human health and well-being, offering a unique perspective on the role of these ideas in shaping our world and our understanding of the universe.

As we explore the many intersections of quantum mechanics with human civilization and the universe, we encourage readers to remain open to the intriguing and sometimes counterintuitive ideas presented in this book. The double-slit experiment serves as a potent reminder that reality may be more complex and mysterious than we initially perceive, and that the pursuit of knowledge often leads us to challenge and reevaluate our most fundamental assumptions about the nature of the world around us.

CHAPTER 27: THE EPR PARADOX AND BELL'S THEOREM

Introduction

In the previous chapter, we discussed the double-slit experiment and its implications for our understanding of the wave-particle duality of matter, the observer effect, and the nature of reality. Another important aspect of quantum mechanics that challenges our classical intuitions and relates to the concepts discussed in the double-slit experiment is the Einstein-Podolsky-Rosen (EPR) paradox and Bell's theorem. In this chapter, we will delve into the history and details of the EPR paradox and Bell's theorem, exploring their significance for quantum mechanics and their connections to the wave-particle duality and observer effect.

The EPR Paradox: A Challenge to Quantum Mechanics

The EPR paradox, named after its authors Albert Einstein, Boris Podolsky, and Nathan Rosen, was first introduced in a 1935 paper as a thought experiment designed to question the completeness of quantum mechanics. The EPR paradox involves two particles that are prepared in a special state known as an entangled state, in which the properties of the particles are correlated with each other. According to the principles of quantum mechanics, the properties of the entangled particles remain undefined until they are measured.

Einstein, Podolsky, and Rosen argued that if the properties of one particle could be instantly determined by measuring the properties of the other particle, even when they are separated by large distances, this would imply a "spooky action at a distance," in which the act of measurement on one particle appears to instantly influence the properties of the other particle. The EPR paradox highlighted a potential conflict between the predictions of quantum mechanics and the principles of locality and realism, which assert that physical processes occurring at one location do not depend on the properties of objects at other locations.

Bell's Theorem: A Resolution to the EPR Paradox

In 1964, physicist John Bell proposed a theorem that offered a resolution to the EPR paradox by demonstrating that the predictions of quantum mechanics are fundamentally incompatible with the assumptions of locality and realism. Bell's theorem shows that if quantum mechanics is correct, then certain correlations between the properties of entangled particles must be stronger than what can be explained by any local, realistic theory.

Numerous experiments have been performed to test the predictions of Bell's theorem, and the results have consistently supported the predictions of quantum mechanics, indicating that the correlations between entangled particles cannot be explained by local, realistic theories. These experimental findings lend further support to the wave-particle duality and the observer effect discussed in the context of the double-slit experiment, as they suggest that the properties of entangled particles are indeed interconnected in a nonlocal manner that defies classical intuition.

Connections to the Double-Slit Experiment

Both the EPR paradox and Bell's theorem, as well as the double-slit experiment, challenge our classical understanding of reality and highlight the counterintuitive nature of quantum mechanics. These concepts emphasize the interconnectedness of quantum systems, the role of observation in determining the properties of particles, and the potential breakdown of locality and realism at the quantum level.

The double-slit experiment demonstrates the wave-particle duality of matter and the observer effect, while the EPR paradox and Bell's theorem reveal the nonlocal correlations between entangled particles. Together, these ideas provide a compelling illustration of the unique and mysterious properties of quantum mechanics, encouraging us to reevaluate our assumptions about the nature of reality and the fundamental principles that govern the universe.

CHAPTER 28: QUANTUM TELEPORTATION AND ITS APPLICATIONS

As we have explored in previous chapters, the double-slit experiment, the EPR paradox, and Bell's theorem have revealed various counterintuitive aspects of quantum mechanics, such as wave-particle duality, the observer effect, and the nonlocal correlations between entangled particles. One fascinating and potentially transformative application of these quantum phenomena is quantum teleportation. In this chapter, we will discuss the concept of quantum teleportation, its theoretical foundations, and its potential applications, while highlighting its connections to the principles discussed in previous chapters.

Quantum Teleportation: A Leap Beyond Classical Boundaries

Quantum teleportation is a process in which the quantum state of a particle is transferred from one location to another without the particle itself traversing the intervening distance. This extraordinary feat is made possible by exploiting the principles of quantum entanglement and superposition, which were discussed in earlier chapters. The process of quantum teleportation involves three main steps:

Entanglement: Two particles are prepared in an entangled state, with one particle (the "helper" particle) being sent to the recipient, while the other particle (the "source" particle) remains with the sender.

Quantum State Measurement: The sender performs a joint measurement on the source particle and the particle whose quantum state is to be teleported. This measurement entangles the two particles, causing the source particle to collapse into a state that is correlated with the quantum state of the particle being teleported.

Quantum State Reconstruction: The sender communicates the results of the joint measurement to the recipient using classical communication channels. The recipient then applies an appropriate quantum operation on the helper particle to reconstruct the original quantum state of the teleported particle.

It is important to note that quantum teleportation does not involve the instantaneous transfer of matter or energy, and it relies on classical communication to transmit the measurement results. This means that quantum teleportation cannot be used to transmit information faster than the speed of light, thus preserving the principles of causality and locality.

Applications of Quantum Teleportation

Quantum teleportation holds significant promise for a wide range of applications, particularly in the fields of quantum communication, quantum computing, and quantum cryptography:

Quantum Communication: Quantum teleportation can be used to transmit quantum information between distant locations, enabling the development of secure and efficient quantum communication networks that are robust against eavesdropping and information loss.

Quantum Computing: In quantum computing, quantum teleportation can serve as a key building block for the implementation of distributed quantum computing architectures and fault-tolerant quantum error correction protocols, potentially revolutionizing our ability to perform complex computations and solve previously intractable problems.

Quantum Cryptography: By leveraging the principles of quantum entanglement and superposition, quantum teleportation can be used to create unconditionally secure communication channels for exchanging cryptographic keys, leading to enhanced security and privacy in the digital age.

Connections to Previous Chapters

Quantum teleportation builds upon the principles of quantum mechanics discussed in previous chapters, such as wave-particle duality, the observer effect, and quantum entanglement. The concept of quantum teleportation relies on the unique properties of entangled particles, which were highlighted in the EPR paradox and Bell's theorem, as well as the wave-particle duality and observer effect demonstrated in the double-slit experiment. By harnessing these quantum phenomena, quantum teleportation has the potential to revolutionize our understanding of communication, computation, and cryptography, opening new horizons for the development of advanced quantum technologies.

In conclusion, quantum teleportation is a remarkable example of the power and potential of quantum mechanics, offering a glimpse into the transformative applications that may emerge from our growing understanding of the quantum world. As we continue to explore the diverse.

and intriguing aspects of quantum mechanics in this book, we are reminded of the far-reaching implications that these ideas have for our understanding of the universe and the technologies that shape our lives. Quantum teleportation is just one of many exciting developments that are emerging from the study of quantum phenomena, paving the way for a future in which the counterintuitive principles of the quantum realm are harnessed to create novel solutions to some of our most pressing challenges.

In the following chapters, we will continue to examine the various ways in which quantum mechanics intersects with human civilization, the universe, and the multiverse. From the quantum mind hypothesis and the role of consciousness in the universe, to the potential applications of quantum mechanics in fields such as medicine, artificial intelligence, and energy production, we will delve into the fascinating possibilities that the quantum world may hold for the future of humanity.

As we navigate this complex and often mysterious terrain, we are continually inspired by the boundless curiosity and innovative spirit that have driven scientific inquiry and discovery throughout human history. By embracing the unknown and pushing the boundaries of our knowledge, we open ourselves to new perspectives and novel insights that can help us to better understand the fundamental nature of reality and our place within it.

CHAPTER 29: QUANTUM SUPERPOSITION AND SCHRÖDINGER'S CAT

Throughout previous chapters, we have discussed various counterintuitive aspects of quantum mechanics, such as wave-particle duality, the observer effect, quantum entanglement, and quantum teleportation. One of the most fundamental and perplexing concepts in quantum mechanics is quantum superposition, which is closely related to the famous thought experiment known as Schrödinger's Cat. In this chapter, we will delve into the concept of quantum superposition, explore the Schrödinger's Cat thought experiment, and discuss their connections to the principles presented in previous chapters. We will also provide an opinion on the significance and implications of these ideas for our understanding of the universe.

Quantum Superposition: A State of Multiple Possibilities

Quantum superposition refers to the principle that quantum particles can exist in multiple states simultaneously until they are measured. This idea arises from the fact that the equations of quantum mechanics, specifically the Schrödinger equation, describe particles not in terms of definite positions or properties, but rather in terms of probability distributions known as wave functions. These wave functions can represent a linear combination of multiple states, indicating that the particle has a certain probability of being found in each state upon measurement.

The act of measurement causes the wave function to collapse, with the particle assuming a single definite state corresponding to the measurement outcome. This phenomenon, known as wave function collapse, is a key aspect of the observer effect discussed in earlier chapters and is closely related to the concept of quantum superposition.

Schrödinger's Cat: A Thought Experiment in Superposition

In 1935, Austrian physicist Erwin Schrödinger proposed a thought experiment to illustrate the seemingly paradoxical implications of quantum superposition for macroscopic objects. Schrödinger's Cat involves placing a cat in a sealed box along with a radioactive atom, a Geiger counter, a vial of poison, and a hammer. If the radioactive atom decays, the Geiger counter detects the decay, causing the hammer to break the vial and release the poison, killing the cat. If the atom does not decay, the cat remains alive.

According to the principles of quantum mechanics, the radioactive atom exists in a superposition of both decayed and undecayed states until it is measured. Consequently, Schrödinger argued that the cat must also exist in a superposition of both alive and dead states until the box is opened and the cat is observed. This thought experiment highlights the seemingly absurd implications of applying quantum superposition to everyday objects and raises important questions about the boundary between the quantum and classical worlds.

Connections to Previous Chapters and Opinion on Significance

Quantum superposition and Schrödinger's Cat are intimately related to the concepts discussed in previous chapters, such as wave-particle duality, the observer effect, and quantum entanglement. These ideas collectively challenge our classical intuitions about reality and underscore the profoundly counterintuitive nature of the quantum world.

In our opinion, the significance of quantum superposition and

Schrödinger's Cat lies not only in their ability to challenge our preconceived notions about the nature of reality, but also in their capacity to inspire further inquiry and discovery in the realm of quantum mechanics. By pushing the boundaries of our understanding and confronting the seemingly paradoxical aspects of the quantum world, we can gain deeper insights into the fundamental principles that govern the universe and develop novel technologies and applications based on these principles.

As we continue to explore the diverse and fascinating landscape of quantum mechanics, we are reminded of the importance of embracing the unknown and questioning our assumptions about the nature of reality. By doing so, we can unlock new perspectives and understanding, opening the door to a future ntinued Exploration and Possibilities

As we continue to explore the various aspects of quantum mechanics, including quantum superposition and Schrödinger's Cat, we are constantly reminded of the vast potential for discovery and innovation that the quantum realm offers. As our understanding of these phenomena deepens, we may uncover new applications and technologies that have the potential to transform human civilization and our understanding of the universe.

Some of the areas in which quantum mechanics is already making an impact include quantum computing, quantum communication, and quantum cryptography, as discussed in previous chapters. The principles of quantum superposition and entanglement are central to these developments, enabling breakthroughs in computational power, secure communication, and data encryption. As we continue to unravel the mysteries of the quantum world, it is likely that we will uncover even more remarkable applications and insights that will shape our future.

In the upcoming chapters, we will delve further into the rich tapestry of quantum mechanics, exploring topics such as the role of quantum mechanics in the multiverse, the nature of time and causality, and the potential impact of quantum mechanics on our understanding of human consciousness and free will. By engaging with these complex and thought-provoking ideas, we invite readers to join us on a journey of discovery and contemplation that transcends the boundaries of classical understanding and offers a glimpse into the extraordinary potential of the quantum world.

CHAPTER 30: RECENT ADVANCES IN QUANTUM EXPERIMENTS

As we have explored in previous chapters, quantum mechanics has led to numerous groundbreaking insights into the nature of reality and the behavior of subatomic particles. These insights have opened up new possibilities for technological advancements and have transformed our understanding of the universe. In this chapter, we will discuss some recent advances in quantum experiments that have further expanded our understanding of the quantum world, while relating these developments to the concepts presented in earlier chapters. By examining the cutting-edge research being conducted in the field of quantum mechanics, we can glimpse the exciting future that lies ahead and the potential impact these discoveries may have on our lives.

Recent Quantum Experiments: Pushing the Boundaries

Quantum Superposition of Large Molecules: One of the most fundamental principles of quantum mechanics, as discussed in Chapter 29, is the concept of quantum superposition. Recent experiments have demonstrated quantum superposition in increasingly large molecules, pushing the limits of our understanding of the boundary between the quantum and classical worlds. These experiments have important implications for our understanding of quantum superposition and the measurement problem, as well as the development of technologies like quantum computing and sensors.

Quantum Entanglement of Macroscopic Objects: Building on the principles of quantum entanglement discussed in earlier chapters, researchers have recently achieved entanglement between macroscopic objects, such as tiny drums and mirrors. These experiments demonstrate the scalability of quantum entanglement and have significant implications for the development of quantum communication networks and quantum computing architectures.

Quantum Teleportation Over Long Distances: As mentioned in Chapter 28, quantum teleportation is a fascinating application of quantum entanglement that allows for the transfer of quantum states between distant locations. Recent experiments have achieved quantum teleportation over increasingly long distances, including through fiber-optic cables and free-space links between satellites and ground stations. These advances bring us closer to the realization of global quantum communication networks and secure quantum internet.

Quantum Simulation of Complex Systems: Quantum simulation is an emerging field that leverages the unique properties of quantum systems to model and simulate complex phenomena that are difficult or impossible to study using classical methods. Recent experiments have successfully used quantum simulators to model challenging problems in areas such as condensed matter physics, high-energy physics, and quantum chemistry. These advances have the potential to revolutionize our understanding of complex systems and lead to new discoveries in materials science, drug development, and fundamental physics.

Quantum Machine Learning and Artificial Intelligence: As discussed in Chapter 24, quantum mechanics plays a significant role in the development of advanced artificial intelligence systems. Researchers have recently made significant progress in developing quantum machine learning algorithms that can outperform their classical counterparts in specific tasks. These advances hold promise for the development of powerful quantum artificial intelligence systems that can tackle previously intractable problems.

Connections to Previous Chapters and Engaging the Reader

These recent advances in quantum experiments build upon the fundamental principles and concepts explored in previous chapters, such as quantum superposition, quantum entanglement, and quantum teleportation. By pushing the boundaries of our understanding of these phenomena, researchers are not only shedding light on the mysteries of the quantum world but also paving the way for transformative applications and technologies that can shape our future.

As a reader, you are invited to witness the unfolding story of quantum mechanics, a story that continues to challenge our understanding of reality and expand the limits of human knowledge. With each new discovery and breakthrough, we gain a deeper appreciation for the richness and complexity of the quantum realm, and we are reminded of the boundless potential for innovation and progress that lies at the heart of scientific inquiry.

In the remaining chapters of this book, we will continue to explore the fascinating world of quantum mechanics, delving into topics such as the implications of quantum theory for our understanding of time and causality, the nature of the multiverse, and the potential impact of quantum mechanics on our understanding of human consciousness and free will. By engaging with these complex and thought-provoking ideas, we hope to provide you with a comprehensive overview of the current state of quantum research and the many possibilities that await us in the future.

As we continue to explore the diverse landscape of quantum mechanics, we encourage you to maintain an open mind and to embrace the counterintuitive and often paradoxical nature of the quantum world. By doing so, you will not only deepen your understanding of the fundamental principles that govern the universe, but you will also become an active participant in the ongoing quest for knowledge and discovery that lies at the heart of scientific progress.

So, as we delve into the remaining chapters of this book, we invite you to join us on this thrilling journey through the quantum realm, a journey that transcends the boundaries of classical understanding and offers a glimpse into the extraordinary potential of the quantum world. Together, we will continue to explore the mysteries of the universe, challenge our preconceptions, and push the limits of human knowledge in pursuit of a deeper understanding of the nature of reality.

PART VII: PHILOSOPHICAL IMPLICATIONS OF QUANTUM MECHANICS

Determinism and Indeterminism
The Nature of Reality and the Role of the Observer
The Problem of Causality in Quantum Mechanics
The Implications of Quantum Mechanics on Time
The Nature of Space and the Quantum Vacuum

CHAPTER 31: DETERMINISM AND INDETERMINISM

In previous chapters, we have explored various aspects of quantum mechanics that challenge our classical understanding of the universe. One such aspect is the question of determinism versus indeterminism in the context of quantum mechanics. In this chapter, we will delve into the philosophical implications of quantum mechanics for our understanding of determinism and indeterminism, and how these concepts relate to the principles of quantum mechanics that we have discussed so far.

Determinism: A Classical Viewpoint

Determinism is the philosophical doctrine that all events, including human actions and decisions, are determined by a chain of prior causes. In other words, if one knows the initial conditions of a system and the laws governing its behavior, one can predict its future state with absolute certainty. This view has its roots in classical physics, which is based on the assumption that the behavior of particles and systems can be described deterministically by Newton's laws of motion and gravitation.

Indeterminism: The Quantum Challenge

In contrast to determinism, indeterminism posits that some events are not determined by prior causes and that there is an inherent unpredictability in the behavior of particles and systems. Quantum mechanics introduces a fundamental indeterminism into our understanding of the universe, as it is based on probabilistic principles rather than deterministic ones. This indeterminism is most famously captured by the

Heisenberg Uncertainty Principle, which states that it is impossible to simultaneously know both the position and momentum of a particle with absolute certainty.

The probabilistic nature of quantum mechanics has led some philosophers and scientists to argue that the universe is fundamentally indeterministic, with chance and uncertainty playing an essential role in the behavior of particles and systems. This view has important implications for our understanding of causality, free will, and the nature of reality, as it challenges the classical deterministic framework upon which these concepts have been traditionally based.

Quantum Mechanics and the Debate between Determinism and Indeterminism

Quantum mechanics has played a crucial role in the ongoing debate between determinism and indeterminism, as it raises several key questions and challenges for both perspectives. Some of the most significant issues include:

Wave Function Collapse and the Measurement Problem: As discussed in earlier chapters, the act of measurement in quantum mechanics causes the wave function to collapse, with the particle assuming a single definite state corresponding to the measurement outcome. This phenomenon raises important questions about the role of the observer in the quantum world and the nature of wave function collapse, which some argue is inherently indeterministic.

Quantum Entanglement and Nonlocality: As we have explored in previous chapters, quantum entanglement and nonlocality challenge the classical notion of causality by demonstrating that the properties of entangled particles can be instantaneously correlated across vast distances. These phenomena have led some to argue that the universe is fundamentally nonlocal and indeterministic, with entangled particles exhibiting a form of "spooky action at a distance."

Interpretations of Quantum Mechanics: Various interpretations of quantum mechanics offer different perspectives on the determinism-indeterminism debate. For example, the Copenhagen interpretation embraces the inherent indeterminism of quantum mechanics, while the Many Worlds Interpretation posits a deterministic multiverse in which all possible outcomes of quantum events are realized.

The question of determinism versus indeterminism is a central philosophical issue that has been significantly influenced by the development of quantum mechanics. By challenging the deterministic principles of classical physics and introducing a fundamental indeterminacy into our understanding of the universe, quantum mechanics has fueled an ongoing debate about the nature of reality, causality, and free will.

As we continue to explore the complex landscape of quantum mechanics in the remaining chapters of this book, we will delve deeper into the philosophical implications of quantum mechanics and consider how these implications may shape our understanding of the nature of the universe and our place within it. We will investigate topics such as the nature of time and causality in the context of quantum mechanics, the role of consciousness in the quantum world, and the potential impact of quantum mechanics on our understanding of human civilization.

By engaging with these complex and thought-provoking ideas, we hope to provide you with a comprehensive overview of the current state of quantum research and the many possibilities that await us in the future. As we continue to uncover the mysteries of the quantum realm, we are not only deepening our understanding of the fundamental principles that govern the universe but also broadening the scope of our philosophical inquiries and inviting new perspectives on age-old questions.

So, as we embark on the remaining chapters of this book, we invite you to join us on this thrilling journey through the quantum realm, a journey that transcends the boundaries of classical understanding and offers a glimpse into the extraordinary potential of the quantum world. Together, we will continue to explore the mysteries of the universe, challenge our preconceptions, and push the limits of human knowledge in pursuit of a deeper understanding of the nature of reality.

The Role of Free Will in the Determinism-Indeterminism Debate

The debate between determinism and indeterminism has important implications for our understanding of free will. If determinism is true, then our actions and decisions are predetermined by a chain of prior causes, which seems to leave little room for free will. On the other hand, if indeterminism is true, then our actions and decisions may be influenced by chance or randomness, which could also be seen as a threat to the concept of free will.

Quantum mechanics adds an additional layer of complexity to this debate, as its probabilistic nature seems to introduce a fundamental element of randomness into the behavior of particles and systems. Some have argued that this indeterminacy could provide a basis for free will, as it allows for the possibility that our actions and decisions are not entirely determined by prior causes.

However, others contend that the indeterminacy of quantum mechanics does not necessarily imply that human actions and decisions are free or uncaused. They argue that even if the behavior of subatomic particles is fundamentally indeterministic, this does not mean that human behavior, which operates at a much larger scale, is also indeterministic. Furthermore, they claim that the existence of randomness or chance at the quantum level does not necessarily provide a basis for free will, as it does not grant us any more control over our actions and decisions.

Ultimately, the question of whether quantum mechanics supports or undermines the concept of free will remains a subject of ongoing debate among philosophers and scientists. As our understanding of quantum mechanics and its implications for determinism and indeterminism continues to evolve, it is likely that this debate will persist, with each new discovery or insight potentially shedding new light on the nature of free will and the limits of human agency.

In conclusion, the debate between determinism and indeterminism is a central philosophical issue that has been significantly influenced by the development of quantum mechanics. The inherent indeterminacy of quantum mechanics has fueled a lively debate about the nature of reality, causality, and free will, and it continues to challenge our understanding of the fundamental principles that govern the universe.

CHAPTER 32: THE NATURE OF REALITY AND THE ROLE OF THE OBSERVER

The nature of reality and the role of the observer are central themes in quantum mechanics that have far-reaching philosophical implications. In this chapter, we will explore these themes in the context of the principles of quantum mechanics discussed in previous chapters and examine how they challenge our classical understanding of reality and the role of the observer in the physical world.

The Nature of Reality in Quantum Mechanics

In classical physics, reality is often thought of as objective and independent of the observer. Objects and systems are believed to have definite properties that exist regardless of whether they are observed or not. However, quantum mechanics introduces a fundamental shift in our understanding of the nature of reality, as it suggests that the properties of particles and systems are not entirely independent of the observer.

As we have seen in previous chapters, the act of measurement in quantum mechanics plays a crucial role in determining the properties of particles and systems. When a quantum system is not being observed, it is described by a wave function that represents a superposition of all possible states. However, upon measurement, the wave function collapses, and the system assumes a single, definite state corresponding to the measurement outcome.

This phenomenon raises important questions about the nature of reality in the quantum world. Is reality fundamentally probabilistic, with particles and systems existing in a superposition of states until observed? Or is there a deeper, deterministic reality that underlies the apparent indeterminacy of quantum mechanics? These questions are at the heart of many ongoing debates and interpretations of quantum mechanics, which we have discussed in previous chapters.

The Role of the Observer

The observer's role in quantum mechanics is closely related to the nature of reality, as the act of measurement influences the properties of particles and systems. This raises important questions about the extent to which the observer shapes reality in the quantum world and whether the observer is an active participant in the creation of reality.

In the Copenhagen interpretation of quantum mechanics, the observer plays a central role in determining the properties of particles and systems. According to this interpretation, the observer's act of measurement causes the wave function to collapse, with the particle assuming a single, definite state that corresponds to the measurement outcome. This view suggests that the observer is an essential component of the quantum world and that reality is, to some extent, dependent on the observer.

However, other interpretations of quantum mechanics, such as the Many Worlds Interpretation, posit a more passive role for the observer. In this view, the observer's act of measurement does not cause the wave function to collapse. Instead, it merely reveals one of the many possible outcomes that exist in a deterministic multiverse.

The nature of reality and the role of the observer in quantum mechanics are central themes that challenge our classical understanding of the physical world. By introducing a fundamental indeterminacy into our understanding of reality and suggesting that the observer plays an active role in shaping the properties of particles and systems, quantum mechanics has fueled ongoing debates about the nature of reality and the observer's role in the universe.

As our understanding of quantum mechanics continues to evolve, these debates are likely to persist, with new discoveries and insights potentially shedding new light on the nature of reality and the observer's role in the quantum world. By engaging with these complex and thought-provoking ideas, we deepen our understanding of the fundamental principles that govern the universe and broaden the scope of our philosophical inquiries.

CHAPTER 33: THE PROBLEM OF CAUSALITY IN QUANTUM MECHANICS

Causality is a foundational concept in classical physics, where the behavior of systems and objects is determined by a chain of prior causes and effects. In this deterministic framework, the future state of a system can be predicted with certainty, given complete information about its initial conditions. However, quantum mechanics introduces a fundamental shift in our understanding of causality, with its inherent probabilistic nature and the apparent influence of the observer on the behavior of particles and systems. In this chapter, we will explore the problem of causality in quantum mechanics and examine how it challenges our classical understanding of cause and effect.

Causality and the Probabilistic Nature of Quantum Mechanics

As we have seen in previous chapters, quantum mechanics is inherently probabilistic, with particles and systems existing in a superposition of states until they are observed or measured. This probabilistic nature of quantum mechanics introduces a fundamental indeterminacy into our understanding of causality, as it implies that the future state of a system cannot be predicted with certainty, even if we have complete information about its initial conditions.

In classical physics, causality is closely related to the concept of determinism, which holds that the behavior of a system is entirely determined by a chain of prior causes and effects. However, the probabilistic nature of quantum mechanics seems to challenge this deterministic view of causality, as it suggests that the behavior of particles and systems is not entirely determined by prior causes but is instead influenced by chance or randomness.

The Role of the Observer in Causality

Another aspect of quantum mechanics that challenges our understanding of causality is the role of the observer in determining the properties of particles and systems. As we have discussed in previous chapters, the act of measurement in quantum mechanics plays a crucial role in the behavior of particles and systems, with the wave function collapsing upon observation and the system assuming a single, definite state.

This phenomenon raises important questions about the nature of causality in the quantum world. Does the observer's act of measurement cause the wave function to collapse, or is the observer merely revealing a preexisting reality? Different interpretations of quantum mechanics, such as the Copenhagen interpretation and the Many Worlds Interpretation, offer different answers to these questions, which we have explored in earlier chapters.

Nonlocality and the EPR Paradox

The problem of causality in quantum mechanics is further complicated by the phenomenon of nonlocality, which we have discussed in previous chapters. Nonlocality, as demonstrated by the EPR paradox and confirmed by experiments such as those based on Bell's theorem, implies that entangled particles can instantaneously affect each other's properties, regardless of the distance between them. This phenomenon seems to violate the principle of locality, which states that physical processes occurring at one location should not have an immediate effect on processes occurring at another location.

The apparent violation of locality by nonlocality raises important questions about the nature of causality in the quantum world. Does nonlocality imply that causality is fundamentally different in the quantum realm, or does it suggest that our understanding of causality needs to be revised to account for these seemingly paradoxical phenomena?

The problem of causality in quantum mechanics is a central issue that challenges our classical understanding of cause and effect. The probabilistic nature of quantum mechanics, the role of the observer in determining the properties of particles and systems, and the phenomenon of nonlocality all introduce complexities and apparent paradoxes that continue to fuel ongoing debates about the nature of causality in the quantum world.

As our understanding of quantum mechanics continues to evolve, it is likely that these debates will persist, with each new discovery or insight potentially shedding new light on the nature of causality and the fundamental principles that govern the universe. By grappling with these complex and thought -provoking ideas, we deepen our understanding of the fundamental principles that govern the universe and broaden the scope of our philosophical inquiries.

Alternative Approaches to Causality in Quantum Mechanics

In response to the challenges posed by quantum mechanics to our classical understanding of causality, some alternative approaches have been proposed to reconcile the apparent contradictions and paradoxes. One such approach is the idea of retrocausality, which suggests that future events can have a causal influence on past events. In this view, the apparent nonlocality of entangled particles could be explained by the influence of future measurements on the past states of the particles.

Another alternative approach is the de Broglie-Bohm interpretation of quantum mechanics, also known as the pilot-wave theory. This interpretation posits that particles are guided by deterministic "pilot waves," which determine their trajectories. In this view, the apparent indeterminacy of quantum mechanics is a result of our limited knowledge of the underlying pilot-wave dynamics, and causality remains deterministic and consistent with classical physics.

It is worth noting that these alternative approaches are still the subject of ongoing debate and have not yet gained consensus among the scientific community. However, they illustrate the richness of thought and exploration surrounding the problem of causality in quantum mechanics.

Implications for Science and Philosophy

The problem of causality in quantum mechanics has far-reaching implications for both science and philosophy. It challenges our understanding of the fundamental principles that underlie the physical world, prompting us to question the very nature of reality and the role of the observer in shaping our experiences. Furthermore, it forces us to confront the limits of our knowledge and the potential limitations of our scientific methods in uncovering the ultimate truths about the universe.

As we continue to probe the mysteries of the quantum world and explore new frontiers in science and technology, it is essential that we remain open to new ideas and perspectives on causality and other foundational concepts. By engaging with the problem of causality in quantum mechanics, we not only expand our understanding of the universe but also contribute to the ongoing dialogue between science and philosophy, which has been instrumental in shaping our intellectual and cultural landscape throughout history.

CHAPTER 34: THE IMPLICATIONS OF QUANTUM MECHANICS ON TIME

Time is a fundamental aspect of our understanding of the universe and the laws that govern it. In classical physics, time is an absolute, independent variable that progresses uniformly, irrespective of the observer or the state of the system. However, quantum mechanics introduces new complexities and challenges to our understanding of time, with its inherent probabilistic nature and the apparent influence of the observer on the behavior of particles and systems. In this chapter, we will explore the implications of quantum mechanics on time, examining the ways in which it challenges our classical understanding of this essential concept and discussing various opinions on the matter.

The Nature of Time in Quantum Mechanics

In classical physics, time is considered to be an independent, continuous variable that flows uniformly in one direction. This understanding of time is consistent with our everyday experience and serves as the foundation for classical mechanics and the deterministic worldview that underlies it.

However, quantum mechanics introduces a fundamentally different perspective on time, with its probabilistic nature and the central role of the observer in determining the properties of particles and systems. In quantum mechanics, time is not an independent variable but rather an integral part of the wave function that describes the state of a quantum system. The evolution of the wave function over time is governed by the Schrödinger equation, which introduces a probabilistic aspect to our understanding of time.

This probabilistic nature of time in quantum mechanics challenges our classical understanding of cause and effect, as we have discussed in the previous chapter. The apparent indeterminacy of quantum mechanics raises questions about the role of time in determining the future states of particles and systems, and whether the concept of time itself needs to be reevaluated in the context of quantum theory.

Time and the Observer

As we have seen in previous chapters, the role of the observer is central to the understanding of quantum mechanics. The act of measurement or observation influences the behavior of particles and systems, causing the wave function to collapse and the system to assume a single, definite state. This phenomenon raises important questions about the relationship between time and the observer in the quantum world.

Does the observer's act of measurement "create" time, as some interpretations of quantum mechanics suggest, or does time exist independently of the observer? Different interpretations of quantum mechanics offer different answers to these questions, which we have explored in earlier chapters.

Time Symmetry and Quantum Mechanics

In classical physics, the laws that govern the behavior of systems and objects are invariant under time reversal, meaning that they remain the same if time were to flow backward instead of forward. This property, known as time symmetry, is a fundamental aspect of classical mechanics and our understanding of cause and effect.

However, the probabilistic nature of quantum mechanics introduces new complexities to the concept of time symmetry. While the Schrödinger equation, which governs the evolution of the wave function, is time-symmetric, the process of wave function collapse upon observation appears to be time-asymmetric, as it leads to a single, definite outcome that is not reversible. This apparent contradiction between the time-symmetric Schrödinger equation and the time-asymmetric process of wave function collapse has been the subject of ongoing debate and research in the field of quantum mechanics.

Opinions on Time and Quantum Mechanics

The implications of quantum mechanics on time have prompted a wide range of opinions and interpretations among physicists and philosophers. Some argue that our classical understanding of time is fundamentally flawed and that a new understanding of time, consistent with the principles of quantum mechanics, is needed. Others propose alternative interpretations of quantum mechanics, such as the de Broglie-Bohm interpretation or the Many Worlds Interpretation, which offer different perspectives on the nature of time in the quantum world.

The implications of quantum mechanics on time are complex and thought -provoking, challenging our classical understanding of this fundamental concept and prompting us to reevaluate our assumptions about the nature of reality. As we continue to explore the mysteries of the quantum world, it is essential that we remain open to new ideas and perspectives on time and other foundational concepts that underlie our understanding of the universe.

The exploration of time in quantum mechanics has far-reaching consequences not only for our understanding of the physical world but also for our philosophical inquiries. Questions about the nature of time, the role of the observer, and the relationship between cause and effect have been at the heart of human thought for centuries, and quantum mechanics has added new layers of complexity to these timeless debates.

As we delve deeper into the quantum realm and develop new

technologies that harness the power of quantum phenomena, it is crucial that we continue to explore the implications of quantum mechanics on time and other fundamental concepts. By engaging with these challenging questions and seeking a deeper understanding of the principles that govern our universe, we not only advance our knowledge of the physical world but also contribute to the ongoing dialogue between science and philosophy that has shaped human thought and culture throughout history.

CHAPTER 35: THE NATURE OF SPACE AND THE QUANTUM VACUUM

The concept of space is fundamental to our understanding of the universe and the laws that govern it. In classical physics, space is considered to be an empty, inert stage upon which particles and fields interact. However, quantum mechanics introduces a new perspective on the nature of space, revealing that it is not as empty or inert as we once believed. In this chapter, we will explore the nature of space in the context of quantum mechanics, focusing on the phenomenon of the quantum vacuum and its implications for our understanding of the universe.

The Quantum Vacuum: A Sea of Virtual Particles

One of the most intriguing aspects of quantum mechanics is the existence of the quantum vacuum. Contrary to classical notions of empty space, the quantum vacuum is not a void but rather a seething sea of virtual particles and fields that are constantly appearing and disappearing due to quantum fluctuations.

These virtual particles are created in pairs, with one particle being the antiparticle of the other. They exist for an extremely short period of time, after which they annihilate each other, returning to the vacuum. These virtual particles and their transient existence have measurable effects on the physical properties of particles and systems, such as the Casimir effect and the Lamb shift.

The quantum vacuum also plays a crucial role in the process

of particle creation and annihilation, which is central to the behavior of elementary particles and the interactions between them. This constant creation and annihilation of virtual particles is responsible for the dynamism and complexity of the quantum world, which is far removed from the static, deterministic picture of classical physics.

The Energy of the Quantum Vacuum

One of the most puzzling aspects of the quantum vacuum is its energy content. According to quantum field theory, the vacuum should have an incredibly large energy density, which arises from the sum of the zero-point energies of all the fields that exist within it. This vacuum energy is sometimes referred to as the cosmological constant, and it plays a crucial role in our understanding of the expansion of the universe.

However, when we attempt to calculate the energy density of the quantum vacuum using known methods, we arrive at a value that is many orders of magnitude larger than what is observed in the universe. This discrepancy, known as the cosmological constant problem, is one of the most significant unresolved issues in modern physics and has profound implications for our understanding of the nature of space and the quantum vacuum.

The Role of the Quantum Vacuum in Cosmology

The quantum vacuum has far-reaching consequences for our understanding of the universe and its evolution. One of the most striking implications of the quantum vacuum is its role in the process of cosmic inflation, which is a theory that explains the rapid expansion of the universe during its early stages.

According to the theory of cosmic inflation, the universe underwent a period of rapid expansion driven by the energy of the quantum vacuum. This expansion smoothed out the distribution of matter and energy in the universe, giving rise to the large-scale structure we observe today. The quantum vacuum also plays a central role in the creation of particles and the formation of structure in the universe, as fluctuations in the vacuum give rise to the seeds of galaxies and other cosmic structures.

Furthermore, the energy of the quantum vacuum is thought to be responsible for the observed accelerated expansion of the universe, which is one of the key pieces of evidence for the existence of dark energy. Understanding the nature of the quantum vacuum and its role in the evolution of the universe is essential for advancing our knowledge of cosmology and the fundamental laws that govern the cosmos.

The nature of space and the quantum vacuum is a fascinating and complex topic that lies at the heart of our understanding of the universe and the laws that govern it. Quantum mechanics reveals that space is not an empty, inert stage but rather a dynamic and active participant in the behavior of particles and fields, constantly teeming with virtual particles and quantum fluctuations.

The quantum vacuum has far-reaching implications for our understanding of the universe, playing a crucial role in phenomena such as cosmic inflation, the creation of particles, and the accelerated expansion of the universe. It also raises fundamental questions about the nature of space itself and challenges our classical assumptions about the emptiness and inertness of the vacuum.

As we continue to explore the mysteries of the quantum world and develop new technologies that harness the power of quantum phenomena, it is essential that we deepen our understanding of the nature of space and the quantum vacuum. By engaging with these complex and challenging questions, we not only advance our knowledge of the physical world but also contribute to the ongoing dialogue between science and philosophy that has shaped human thought and culture throughout history.

Future research into the nature of space and the quantum vacuum may yield new insights into the fundamental laws of the universe and pave the way for a more complete and coherent understanding of the cosmos. As we push the boundaries of our knowledge and explore the furthest reaches of the quantum world, we open ourselves to the possibility of discovering new principles and phenomena that will enrich our understanding of the universe and the laws that govern it.

PART VIII: THEORIES UNITING QUANTUM MECHANICS AND RELATIVITY

The Quest for Quantum Gravity
Loop Quantum Gravity
String Theory and M-Theory
Holographic Principle and the Black Hole Information Paradox
The Future of Unifying Theories

CHAPTER 36: THE QUEST FOR QUANTUM GRAVITY

One of the greatest challenges in modern theoretical physics is the search for a theory that unifies quantum mechanics and general relativity, the two most successful and well-tested theories in the history of science. While quantum mechanics has been spectacularly successful in describing the behavior of particles and forces at the atomic and subatomic scales, general relativity provides an equally successful framework for understanding the force of gravity and the large-scale structure of the universe. However, these two theories are fundamentally incompatible, and the quest for a unified theory that reconciles them, known as quantum gravity, has been a central focus of research for decades.

The Problem of Unification

The incompatibility between quantum mechanics and general relativity arises from their fundamentally different descriptions of space, time, and the nature of physical phenomena. General relativity is a classical theory that describes gravity as the curvature of spacetime caused by the presence of mass and energy. In this framework, space and time are continuous and smooth, and physical processes are described by smooth, deterministic equations.

On the other hand, quantum mechanics is an inherently probabilistic theory that describes particles and fields in terms of wavefunctions and probabilities. In the quantum world, space and time are discrete, and physical processes are described by probabilistic equations that exhibit inherent uncertainties and discontinuities.

These fundamental differences between the two theories present a major challenge for unification efforts. For instance, the smooth spacetime of general relativity is at odds with the discrete, probabilistic nature of quantum mechanics, and attempts to quantize gravity by treating it as a force similar to the other fundamental forces have been plagued by mathematical difficulties and inconsistencies.

Approaches to Quantum Gravity

There have been several major approaches to quantum gravity, each with its own set of challenges and successes. Some of the most well-known approaches include:

String Theory: String theory is a theoretical framework that posits that the fundamental constituents of the universe are not point-like particles but rather one-dimensional strings. These strings vibrate at different frequencies, giving rise to the various particles and forces observed in the universe. String theory has the potential to unify quantum mechanics and general relativity by replacing the concept of point particles with strings, which can exist in a continuous spacetime while still exhibiting quantum mechanical properties.

Loop Quantum Gravity: Loop quantum gravity is another prominent approach to quantum gravity that seeks to reconcile the discreteness of quantum mechanics with the continuous nature of spacetime. In this framework, space and time are represented by discrete loops and networks, which provide a natural way to incorporate the probabilistic nature of quantum mechanics into the fabric of spacetime itself.

Quantum Field Theory in Curved Spacetime: This approach involves adapting the techniques of quantum field theory, which have been successful in describing the other fundamental forces, to the curved spacetime of general relativity. Although this approach has provided valuable insights into the behavior of quantum fields in the presence of gravity, it has not yet produced a fully consistent and complete theory of quantum gravity.

Other Approaches: There are many other approaches to quantum gravity, including emergent gravity, causal set theory, and asymptotically safe gravity, among others. Each of these approaches has its own unique insights and challenges, and it is possible that a successful theory of quantum gravity may incorporate elements from multiple approaches.

The Implications of Quantum Gravity

A successful theory of quantum gravity would have far-reaching implications for our understanding of the universe and the laws that govern it. It would not only provide a unified framework for describing all known particles and forces, but it could also shed light on some of the most profound mysteries in modern physics, such as the nature of dark matter and dark energy, the origin of the universe, and the ultimate fate of black holes and spacetime singularities.

Moreover, a unified theory of quantum gravity could lead to the development of new technologies and applications, as has been the case with previous breakthroughs in physics. For instance, the unification of electricity and magnetism in the 19th century led to the development of electric generators, motors, and the entire field of electronics, while the development of quantum mechanics in the 20th century paved the way for technologies such as transistors, lasers, and quantum computers.

Some potential applications of a successful quantum gravity theory could include:

Harnessing gravitational waves: With a deeper understanding of quantum gravity, we might be able to develop new ways to detect and manipulate gravitational waves, which could have applications in communication, navigation, and energy production.

Exploring higher dimensions: If a quantum gravity theory requires the existence of extra dimensions, as in string theory, we might be able to explore these dimensions and develop new technologies based on the properties of higher-dimensional physics.

Probing the early universe: A successful theory of quantum gravity could help us understand the conditions that existed in the early universe, potentially shedding light on the origin of matter, the formation of galaxies, and the nature of dark matter and dark energy.

Conclusion

The quest for quantum gravity represents one of the most significant and challenging endeavors in modern physics. Despite the difficulties and complexities involved in reconciling quantum mechanics and general relativity, researchers continue to explore new ideas and approaches in the hope of achieving a deeper understanding of the fundamental laws that govern the universe.

As we push the boundaries of our knowledge and seek to unify the seemingly disparate realms of the quantum and the cosmological, we are not only advancing our understanding of the cosmos but also enriching the human experience and expanding our collective imagination. The pursuit of quantum gravity is not only a testament to the power of human curiosity and ingenuity but also a reminder of the profound beauty and mystery that lie at the heart of the natural world.

CHAPTER 37: LOOP QUANTUM GRAVITY

Loop Quantum Gravity (LQG) is a leading approach to developing a quantum theory of gravity, which aims to reconcile the incompatibility between quantum mechanics and general relativity. This approach provides a non-perturbative, background-independent description of the quantum structure of spacetime by combining elements of both theories. In LQG, the fabric of spacetime is represented by networks of loops, which embody both the discrete nature of quantum mechanics and the continuous spacetime structure of general relativity.

Foundations of Loop Quantum Gravity

The key idea underlying LQG is that spacetime can be described by a network of loops, with each loop corresponding to a discrete unit of area or volume. These loops are formed by the action of quantum operators on a state of the gravitational field, resulting in a quantized geometric structure. This quantized structure of spacetime is fundamentally different from the smooth, continuous spacetime of general relativity, but it provides a natural way to incorporate the discreteness of quantum mechanics into the fabric of spacetime.

LQG is built on two main mathematical structures: spin networks and spin foams. Spin networks are graphs that represent the quantum state of the gravitational field, with edges carrying quantum numbers corresponding to discrete areas and vertices corresponding to discrete volumes. Spin foams, on the other hand, are higher-dimensional analogs of spin networks that describe the evolution of the quantum state of the gravitational field over time.

Dynamics and Evolution in Loop Quantum Gravity

One of the central challenges in LQG is to describe the dynamics and evolution of the quantum state of the gravitational field. This requires defining a quantum version of the Hamiltonian constraint, which is the key equation governing the evolution of the gravitational field in general relativity. In LQG, this constraint takes the form of a complicated operator that acts on the quantum state of the gravitational field, leading to the formation and evolution of spin networks and spin foams.

Several proposals have been put forward for defining the Hamiltonian constraint in LQG, but a complete and consistent formulation of the dynamics remains an open problem. Recent progress has been made in developing techniques for calculating the evolution of spin networks and spin foams, and these developments have shed light on the possible emergence of classical spacetime from the underlying quantum structure.

The Role of Loop Quantum Gravity in Cosmology

LQG has important implications for our understanding of the early universe and the nature of cosmological singularities, such as the Big Bang and black hole singularities. In particular, the discrete structure of spacetime in LQG suggests that the singularity at the Big Bang may be replaced by a "bounce" in which the universe contracts to a minimum size before expanding again.

This idea has given rise to a new field of research known as Loop Quantum Cosmology (LQC), which applies the techniques and insights of LQG to the study of the early universe. LQC has led to several novel predictions about the behavior of the universe near the Big Bang, including a possible explanation for the observed homogeneity and isotropy of the cosmic microwave background radiation.

Challenges and Open Questions

Despite the progress that has been made in developing LQG, there are still several major challenges and open questions that remain to be addressed. These include:

The problem of dynamics: As mentioned earlier, a complete and consistent formulation of the dynamics of LQG remains an open problem. Developing a consistent and physically meaningful definition of the Hamiltonian constraint is crucial for understanding the evolution of the quantum state of the gravitational field and the emergence of classical spacetime.

The semiclassical limit: One of the key challenges in LQG is to show how the discrete quantum structure of spacetime gives rise to the smooth , continuous spacetime of general relativity in the appropriate limit. This semiclassical limit is essential for understanding how classical physics emerges from the underlying quantum structure and for connecting the predictions of LQG with observational data.

The unification of forces: Although LQG provides a framework for incorporating quantum mechanics into the description of spacetime, it does not directly address the unification of gravity with the other fundamental forces of nature, such as electromagnetism and the strong and weak nuclear forces. Integrating LQG with a more comprehensive theory of quantum gravity, possibly within the context of string theory or another approach, remains an important goal.

The experimental validation: One of the major challenges facing any theory of quantum gravity is the difficulty of testing its predictions experimentally. Due to the extremely small scales and energies involved in quantum gravity phenomena, direct experimental tests are currently beyond the reach of our technology. However, there may be indirect ways to probe the predictions of LQG, such as through the observation of cosmic microwave background radiation or the behavior of black holes.

Loop Quantum Gravity is a promising approach to developing a quantum theory of gravity that incorporates both the discreteness of quantum mechanics and the continuous spacetime structure of general relativity. Although significant progress has been made in understanding the mathematical foundations and physical implications of LQG, several major challenges and open questions remain to be addressed. As researchers continue to explore the rich and complex landscape of LQG, they are not only deepening our understanding of the fundamental nature of spacetime but also pushing the boundaries of human knowledge and our capacity to comprehend the mysteries of the universe.

CHAPTER 38: STRING THEORY AND M-THEORY

String theory and M-theory are among the most promising and well-known approaches to developing a unified theory of quantum gravity. String theory proposes that the fundamental building blocks of the universe are not point-like particles but one-dimensional, vibrating strings. This idea has led to a rich mathematical framework and a multitude of theoretical insights, which have inspired a wide range of research across various fields of physics. M-theory, a more general framework that includes string theory, extends the concept of strings to higher-dimensional objects known as branes and posits a deeper structure that encompasses all known string theories.

Foundations of String Theory

At its core, string theory replaces the notion of point-like particles with one-dimensional strings as the fundamental constituents of the universe. These strings can be either open (with two endpoints) or closed (forming a loop), and they vibrate at different frequencies, which determine their properties such as mass and charge. The vibrational patterns of these strings give rise to the various particles and forces observed in nature.

One of the key features of string theory is the requirement of extra dimensions beyond the familiar three dimensions of space and one dimension of time. In order to maintain mathematical consistency, string theory requires a total of 10 spacetime dimensions, which implies the existence of six additional, compactified dimensions. These extra dimensions can take various shapes, known as Calabi-Yau manifolds, which have a profound impact on the properties of strings and the resulting low-energy physics.

M-Theory: Unifying the String Theories

In the mid-1990s, it was discovered that the various versions of string theory were, in fact, different aspects of a more general and encompassing framework called M-theory. M-theory unifies the five known string theories and introduces higher-dimensional objects called branes, which can have anywhere from zero to nine spatial dimensions. In M-theory, strings can be viewed as one-dimensional branes, and the theory itself is thought to exist in 11 spacetime dimensions.

The precise nature and structure of M-theory remain elusive, but its existence has led to many important insights and conjectures, such as the AdS/CFT correspondence, which relates string theory in a curved spacetime to a lower-dimensional quantum field theory. This correspondence has profound implications for our understanding of quantum gravity and the nature of spacetime itself.

String Theory and Quantum Gravity

String theory provides a natural framework for incorporating quantum mechanics into the description of gravity. In this context, the graviton, the hypothetical particle responsible for mediating the gravitational force, emerges as a particular vibrational mode of a closed string. By replacing point-like particles with strings, string theory avoids the problem of non-renormalizability that plagues conventional quantum gravity approaches, such as perturbative attempts to quantize general relativity.

In addition to its potential as a quantum theory of gravity, string theory has also led to important insights into various aspects of particle physics, such as supersymmetry, gauge theory dynamics, and the unification of forces. These connections have opened up new avenues of research and inspired many physicists to explore the rich and intricate landscape of string theory and its applications.

Challenges and Open Questions

Despite its numerous successes and insights, string theory still faces several major challenges and open questions, including:

The landscape problem: The existence of a vast number of possible solutions, or vacua, within string theory, collectively referred to as the "landscape," raises questions about the uniqueness and predictability of the theory. Determining the specific vacuum that describes our universe and understanding the principles that govern this selection remain open questions.

Experimental validation: Like other approaches to quantum gravity, string theory faces the challenge of finding experimental evidence to support its predictions . The small scales and energies involved in quantum gravity phenomena make direct experimental tests extremely difficult with current technology. However, there may be indirect ways to probe the predictions of string theory, such as through the observation of cosmic microwave background radiation, the search for supersymmetric particles, or the study of black holes and gravitational waves.

Connection to the real world: Although string theory provides a mathematically consistent framework for unifying gravity with the other fundamental forces, it has yet to provide a complete and detailed description of the particles and interactions observed in nature. Establishing a clear and concrete connection between string theory and the standard model of particle physics is a crucial step in validating the theory as a true description of the fundamental structure of the universe.

The nature of M-theory: The precise structure and formulation of M-theory, which unifies the various string theories and extends the concept to higher-dimensional objects, remain mysterious. Understanding the deeper principles and mathematical underpinnings of M-theory is an ongoing challenge, which could potentially reveal new insights into the nature of spacetime, quantum gravity, and the unification of forces.

String theory and M-theory represent a vast and intricate framework that aims to provide a unified description of quantum gravity and the fundamental forces of nature. Although these theories have produced a wealth of theoretical insights and connections, many challenges and open questions remain to be addressed. As physicists continue to explore the rich landscape of string theory, they are not only pushing the boundaries of human knowledge but also seeking to unveil the deepest mysteries of the universe and the ultimate nature of reality.

CHAPTER 39: HOLOGRAPHIC PRINCIPLE AND THE BLACK HOLE INFORMATION PARADOX

The holographic principle and the black hole information paradox are two closely related concepts that have emerged from the interplay of quantum mechanics, general relativity, and thermodynamics. These ideas have not only deepened our understanding of the fundamental nature of space, time, and information but also revealed profound connections between seemingly disparate areas of physics.

The Holographic Principle

The holographic principle is a theoretical conjecture that states that the information contained within a region of space can be fully described by a set of data encoded on its boundary. This idea was inspired by the study of black holes and their thermodynamic properties, which led to the realization that the entropy of a black hole is proportional to the area of its event horizon, rather than its volume. This surprising result suggests that the information content of a system is fundamentally constrained by its surface area, rather than its volume.

One of the most celebrated realizations of the holographic principle is the AdS/CFT correspondence, which was discovered in the context of string theory and M-theory. This correspondence relates a gravitational theory in a higher-dimensional, negatively curved spacetime (called anti-de Sitter space) to a lower-dimensional quantum field theory defined on the boundary of that space. The AdS/CFT correspondence provides a powerful framework for understanding various aspects of quantum gravity, including black holes, spacetime singularities, and the emergence of spacetime itself from more fundamental degrees of freedom.

The Black Hole Information Paradox

The black hole information paradox is a longstanding puzzle that arises from the apparent conflict between general relativity, quantum mechanics, and the principles of thermodynamics. According to general relativity, a black hole forms when a massive object collapses under its own gravity, leading to the formation of an event horizon from which nothing, not even light, can escape. From the perspective of an external observer, any information that falls into a black hole is lost forever.

However, in the 1970s, Stephen Hawking discovered that black holes are not truly black but instead emit radiation due to quantum effects near the event horizon. This radiation, known as Hawking radiation, causes the black hole to evaporate over time, eventually disappearing completely. The paradox arises from the fact that Hawking radiation appears to be completely thermal and carries no information about the initial state of the black hole, which seems to imply that information is irretrievably lost when a black hole evaporates. This conclusion is in conflict with the fundamental principles of quantum mechanics, which require that information must be conserved in any physical process.

Resolving the Paradox

The resolution of the black hole information paradox has been a major challenge in theoretical physics for several decades. One promising approach to resolving the paradox is the holographic principle and the AdS/CFT correspondence, which provide a new perspective on the nature of black holes and the flow of information in and out of them.

In this framework, the information that falls into a black hole is not truly lost but is instead encoded on the event horizon, which acts as a holographic screen that stores the information in a highly scrambled form. As the black hole evaporates through Hawking radiation, the information encoded on the horizon is gradually released back into the surrounding spacetime, preserving the unitarity of the quantum mechanical evolution.

The holographic principle and the black hole information paradox are deeply interconnected ideas that have significantly advanced our understanding of the fundamental nature of spacetime, information, and the interplay between quantum mechanics and gravity. These concepts have not only revealed surprising connections between different areas of physics but have also provided important clues about the ultimate structure of the universe and the nature of reality itself.

CHAPTER 40: THE FUTURE OF UNIFYING THEORIES

Unifying theories have always been a central goal in the pursuit of understanding the fundamental nature of the universe. From the earliest days of science, physicists have sought to explain diverse phenomena under a single, comprehensive framework. Quantum mechanics and general relativity represent our current understanding of the microscopic and macroscopic realms, respectively. However, despite their remarkable success in describing a wide range of physical phenomena, these two theories remain fundamentally incompatible. The search for a unified theory that can seamlessly merge quantum mechanics and general relativity has been an ongoing endeavor for many decades, and the future of unifying theories will undoubtedly play a crucial role in shaping our understanding of the universe.

Current Candidates for Unification

String Theory and M-Theory: String theory is perhaps the most well-known candidate for a unifying theory, providing a framework that naturally incorporates both quantum mechanics and general relativity. In string theory, the fundamental constituents of the universe are one-dimensional strings rather than point particles. M-theory, an extension of string theory, unifies all five known string theories and includes higher-dimensional objects called branes.

Loop Quantum Gravity: Another promising candidate for unification is loop quantum gravity (LQG). LQG is a non-perturbative approach to quantum gravity that quantizes spacetime itself, representing it as a network of interacting loops. Although LQG and string theory differ in their approaches, they both aim to reconcile general relativity with quantum mechanics.

Future Directions in Unifying Theories

Experimental Tests: One of the greatest challenges for any unifying theory is to make testable predictions that can be verified experimentally. As technology continues to advance, it is possible that new experimental techniques will emerge that could provide indirect evidence for these theories, such as the detection of supersymmetric particles, the observation of extra dimensions, or the precise measurement of gravitational waves.

Theoretical Developments: As our understanding of both quantum mechanics and general relativity continues to evolve, new theoretical breakthroughs may provide fresh insights into the fundamental nature of reality. These breakthroughs could lead to the discovery of new principles or symmetries that could guide the development of a successful unifying theory.

Interdisciplinary Connections: The search for a unified theory has already led to unexpected connections between various branches of physics, such as the AdS/CFT correspondence in string theory and the holographic principle. It is likely that future developments in unifying theories will continue to draw upon insights from diverse areas of science, from cosmology and particle physics to information theory and condensed matter physics.

Alternative Theories: While string theory and loop quantum gravity are currently the most prominent candidates for unifying quantum mechanics and general relativity, it is possible that a completely new framework could emerge that surpasses both of these approaches. The history of science has often been marked by unexpected discoveries and paradigm shifts, and the search for a unified theory is no exception.

The future of unifying theories holds immense promise, as physicists continue to explore the frontiers of knowledge in the quest to understand the fundamental nature of the universe. Regardless of whether a successful unification is achieved through string theory, loop quantum gravity, or an entirely new framework, the pursuit of a unified understanding of the cosmos will undoubtedly continue to drive the progress of science and expand the boundaries of human knowledge.

PART IX: POPULAR SCIENCE AND QUANTUM MECHANICS

Quantum Mechanics in Science Fiction
Movies and TV Shows Exploring Quantum Mechanics
The Role of Quantum Mechanics in Art and Design
Quantum Mechanics in Everyday Life
Debunking Common Quantum Misconceptions

CHAPTER 41: QUANTUM MECHANICS IN SCIENCE FICTION

Quantum mechanics, with its counterintuitive principles and mind-bending implications, has long captured the imaginations of science fiction writers and readers alike. The unique properties of the quantum world, such as wave-particle duality, superposition, and entanglement, have served as fertile ground for countless imaginative stories that explore the boundaries of scientific possibility. In this chapter, we delve into the ways in which quantum mechanics has been utilized in science fiction, from classic works to modern masterpieces, and examine how these narratives have influenced our understanding of the quantum realm and its potential applications.

Pioneering Works in Quantum Science Fiction

"The Golden Man" (1954) by Philip K. Dick: One of the earliest science fiction stories to incorporate quantum mechanics, "The Golden Man" tells the story of a mutant with the ability to perceive all possible futures and choose the one most beneficial to him. This concept draws on the idea of quantum superposition, where particles exist in multiple states simultaneously until observed.

"The Many Worlds of Hugh Everett III" (1970) by Bryce DeWitt: Inspired by the physicist Hugh Everett III's many-worlds interpretation of quantum mechanics, DeWitt's short story explores the idea of parallel universes generated by quantum events. The protagonist is a researcher who discovers the ability to traverse between these alternate realities, experiencing the vastly different outcomes that arise from seemingly insignificant decisions.

Quantum Mechanics in Modern Science Fiction

"Schrodinger's Cat Trilogy" (1979-1981) by Robert Anton Wilson: This satirical series uses the famous thought experiment of Schrödinger's cat as a metaphor for the uncertainty and paradoxes that permeate the narrative. The trilogy incorporates quantum mechanics, parallel universes, and other advanced concepts to create a wildly imaginative, thought-provoking, and often humorous exploration of reality.

"Quantum Thief Trilogy" (2010-2014) by Hannu Rajaniemi: Set in a far-future solar system, this series follows the adventures of a post-human thief and his exploits in a world where quantum technology has become ubiquitous. The novels incorporate concepts such as quantum entanglement, cryptography, and teleportation, while exploring themes of identity, memory, and the nature of consciousness.

Quantum Mechanics and Time Travel

One of the most popular applications of quantum mechanics in science fiction is the concept of time travel. The indeterminacy of quantum events has led to numerous stories that explore the possibility of altering the past, the consequences of changing the future, and the paradoxes that arise from such endeavors. Some notable examples include:

"The End of Eternity" (1955) by Isaac Asimov: This classic novel centers around a secret organization that uses time travel to manipulate history for the betterment of humanity. The story delves into the complexities of causality and the potentially disastrous consequences of tampering with the past.

"The Chronoliths" (2001) by Robert Charles Wilson: When mysterious monuments from the future begin appearing around the world, the protagonist is drawn into a race against time to decipher their meaning and prevent a potential catastrophe. The novel explores themes of determinism, free will, and the ethical implications of knowing the future.

Quantum mechanics has served as a rich source of inspiration for science fiction writers, providing a framework for exploring the limits of human understanding and the potential of emerging technologies. The imaginative tales spun by these authors not only entertain and captivate readers but also encourage us to ponder the implications of our evolving understanding of the universe. As our knowledge of the quantum world continues to grow, it is likely that the interplay between quantum mechanics and science Fiction will continue to deepen, offering new insights and possibilities for storytellers and audiences alike.

Quantum Mechanics and Virtual Reality

The strange properties of the quantum realm have also inspired science fiction narratives that delve into the world of virtual reality and simulated universes. By harnessing the power of quantum computing, these stories explore the potential for creating immersive, indistinguishable-from-reality experiences that raise questions about the nature of existence and the boundaries between the real and the virtual. Some notable examples include:

"Permutation City" (1994) by Greg Egan: In this novel, a powerful quantum computer enables the creation of fully simulated universes, inhabited by digital copies of human minds. The story raises profound questions about the nature of consciousness, the ethics of creating simulated beings, and the possibility of achieving immortality through digital means.

"The Quantum Rose" (2000) by Catherine Asaro: This Nebula Award-winning novel incorporates elements of quantum mechanics in its depiction of a virtual reality world where users can manipulate their environment through their thoughts. The story explores the potential consequences of such technology, including addiction, the loss of personal identity, and the blurring of the lines between the virtual and the real.

Quantum Mechanics and the Nature of Consciousness

The intersection of quantum mechanics and the nature of consciousness has also been a popular theme in science fiction. These stories often delve into the idea that consciousness may play a fundamental role in the fabric of the universe, as suggested by some interpretations of quantum mechanics. Examples of such works include:

"The Mind's I" (1981) by Douglas Hofstadter and Daniel Dennett: This collection of essays and short stories explores the relationship between consciousness and quantum mechanics, touching upon topics such as the observer effect, the role of consciousness in collapsing the wave function, and the potential existence of a "quantum mind."

"Blindsight" (2006) by Peter Watts: Set in a future where humanity encounters an enigmatic extraterrestrial species, this novel delves into the nature of consciousness and its potential connection to quantum mechanics. The story raises questions about the true nature of intelligence, the limits of human understanding, and the possibility of non-conscious beings that can still interact with the quantum world.

In conclusion, the exploration of quantum mechanics in science fiction has provided a wealth of thought-provoking and imaginative stories that challenge our understanding of reality, time, consciousness, and the very fabric of the universe. As our knowledge of the quantum realm continues to expand, it is likely that science fiction will continue to push the boundaries of what is possible, inspiring future generations of scientists and readers alike.

CHAPTER 42: MOVIES AND TV SHOWS EXPLORING QUANTUM MECHANICS

Quantum mechanics, with its enigmatic principles and intriguing implications, has not only captivated the minds of writers but has also inspired numerous movies and television shows. Film and television creators have utilized the concepts of quantum mechanics to tell stories that explore the boundaries of scientific possibility, often blending fiction and fact to create visually stunning and intellectually stimulating narratives. In this chapter, we will examine some of the most influential and thought-provoking movies and TV shows that have delved into the realm of quantum mechanics.

Movies Featuring Quantum Mechanics

"A Wrinkle in Time" (1962, 2018): Based on the classic novel by Madeleine L'Engle, this story revolves around a young girl's journey through space and time, guided by three mysterious beings. The film uses the concept of a "tesseract," which is a higher-dimensional analogue of a cube, as a means of exploring the possibilities of space-time travel and the existence of parallel universes.

"What the Bleep Do We Know!?" (2004): This hybrid documentary-fiction film delves into the mysterious world of quantum mechanics, blending scientific explanations, animated sequences, and a fictional narrative to explore the connection between quantum physics, consciousness, and reality. The film has generated much discussion and debate, both for its presentation of scientific concepts and its philosophical implications.

"Primer" (2004): This independent science fiction film tells the story of two engineers who inadvertently create a time machine in their garage. The movie explores the consequences of time travel and the moral dilemmas that arise from manipulating the past, all while incorporating concepts from quantum mechanics and theoretical physics.

"Interstellar" (2014): Directed by Christopher Nolan, this visually stunning film explores the concept of time dilation and the effects of gravity on space-time. The movie follows a group of astronauts who embark on a journey through a wormhole in search of a new home for humanity, encountering black holes, higher dimensions, and the paradoxes of time travel along the way.

TV Shows Incorporating Quantum Mechanics

"Quantum Leap" (1989-1993): This classic television series follows the adventures of a scientist who becomes trapped in a time-travel experiment, "leaping" into the bodies of different people throughout history. The show uses the concept of quantum mechanics to explore the nature of time, reality, and the consequences of changing the past.

"Fringe" (2008-2013): This science fiction television series delves into the world of "fringe" science, including quantum mechanics, parallel universes, and alternate realities. The show's characters investigate strange phenomena and uncover a larger conspiracy involving the collision of two parallel worlds.

"Devs" (2020): This limited series, created by Alex Garland, centers around a secretive quantum computing company and the mysterious death of an employee. The show explores themes of determinism, free will, and the implications of advanced quantum computing technology on the nature of reality and human existence.

"Dark" (2017-2020): This German-language Netflix series

revolves around the disappearance of several children in a small town, which is revealed to be connected to time travel and the existence of multiple, interconnected realities. The show incorporates elements of quantum mechanics, such as the many-worlds interpretation and the bootstrap paradox, to create a complex and engrossing narrative.

Movies and television shows have embraced the fascinating world of quantum mechanics, utilizing its concepts and implications to tell stories that captivate audiences and stimulate intellectual curiosity. These narratives not only entertain but also encourage viewers to consider the deeper questions posed by our understanding of the quantum realm and its potential impact on our perception of reality, consciousness, and the nature of the universe. As our understanding of quantum mechanics continues to evolve, it is likely that filmmakers and television creators will continue to be inspired by its enigmatic principles, leading to new and innovative stories that push the boundaries of imagination and challenge our preconceived notions of what is possible.

Furthermore, these movies and television shows serve as an essential bridge between the scientific community and the general public. By presenting complex scientific concepts in an engaging and accessible manner, these narratives help to demystify quantum mechanics, making it more approachable for a wider audience. This not only promotes scientific literacy but also fosters a greater appreciation for the beauty and wonder of the natural world.

In the future, we can expect even more groundbreaking movies and TV shows that incorporate quantum mechanics, as filmmakers and showrunners continue to explore the potential narrative possibilities offered by this fascinating branch of science. With the rapid advancements in quantum technology and our understanding of the quantum realm, there is no shortage of captivating stories to be told, and audiences can look forward to a new era of thought-provoking and visually stunning films and series that delve into the very heart of the quantum universe.

CHAPTER 43: THE ROLE OF QUANTUM MECHANICS IN ART AND DESIGN

The mysterious and fascinating world of quantum mechanics has not only inspired movies, television shows, and literature but has also had a profound impact on the fields of art and design. Artists and designers have drawn inspiration from the principles and concepts of quantum mechanics, creating works that visually and conceptually explore the enigmatic nature of the quantum realm. In this chapter, we will examine how quantum mechanics has influenced art and design and highlight some notable examples of quantum-inspired creations.

Quantum Mechanics as a Source of Inspiration

The complex and counterintuitive principles of quantum mechanics, such as wave-particle duality, quantum entanglement, and superposition, challenge our traditional understanding of reality and offer a wealth of creative inspiration for artists and designers. By incorporating these concepts into their work, they are able to push the boundaries of artistic expression and create innovative and thought-provoking pieces that encourage viewers to contemplate the nature of reality, the universe, and their place within it.

Notable Examples of Quantum-Inspired Art and Design

Julian Voss-Andreae: A former physicist turned artist, Voss-Andreae creates sculptures that draw inspiration from the principles of quantum mechanics. His works often incorporate materials such as steel and glass to create visually striking, abstract forms that reflect the elusive and paradoxical nature of the quantum realm. One of his most famous pieces, "Quantum Man," is a life-sized sculpture of a walking man made from parallel steel sheets, which appears to vanish from certain angles, reflecting the concept of quantum superposition.

Joma Sipe: This Portuguese artist creates intricate, geometric works inspired by the concepts of quantum mechanics and sacred geometry. Sipe's paintings often feature complex, symmetrical patterns that evoke the idea of a quantum wave function, representing the probabilistic nature of particles in the quantum realm. His work encourages viewers to contemplate the interconnectedness of all things and the underlying mathematical structure of the universe.

Semiconductor: The British art duo Ruth Jarman and Joe Gerhardt, known as Semiconductor, create visually captivating films and installations that explore the invisible world of quantum mechanics. Their works often utilize scientific data and computer simulations to create immersive visual and sonic experiences that give audiences a glimpse into the quantum realm. Their 2018 installation, "HALO," uses data from the Large Hadron Collider at CERN to create a mesmerizing audiovisual representation of subatomic particle collisions.

Lia Halloran: An artist and astrophysicist, Halloran creates paintings and installations that explore the intersection of art, science, and the cosmos. Her work often incorporates elements of quantum mechanics, such as particle tracks and wave patterns, creating visually striking images that evoke the enigmatic nature of the quantum world. Halloran's art encourages viewers to contemplate the beauty and complexity of the universe and our place within it.

Quantum mechanics has provided artists and designers with a rich source of inspiration, enabling them to create innovative and thought-provoking works that challenge our understanding of reality and the nature of the universe. By incorporating the principles and concepts of quantum mechanics into their creations, these artists and designers not only push the boundaries of artistic expression but also encourage a greater appreciation for the beauty and complexity of the natural world.

As our understanding of the quantum realm continues to evolve, it is likely that artists and designers will continue to be inspired by its enigmatic properties, leading to new and groundbreaking works that explore the mysteries of the universe and our place within it. Through their art, these creators help to bridge the gap between the scientific community and the general public, fostering a greater appreciation for the wonders of the quantum world and inspiring a new generation of artists and scientists alike.

CHAPTER 44: QUANTUM MECHANICS IN EVERYDAY LIFE

While quantum mechanics may seem like an abstract and highly complex branch of science, its principles and applications have a significant impact on our everyday lives. The development of modern technologies and innovations can be traced back to our understanding of quantum phenomena. In this chapter, we will explore some of the ways in which quantum mechanics has influenced and shaped the world around us and discuss the everyday technologies that rely on quantum principles.

Electronics and Semiconductors
One of the most significant applications of quantum mechanics in daily life is in the field of electronics. The invention of the transistor and the subsequent development of semiconductor technology were made possible by our understanding of quantum mechanics. These innovations form the basis of modern electronics, including smartphones, computers, and other digital devices that have become essential components of our everyday lives.

GPS Navigation
The Global Positioning System (GPS) technology, which provides accurate location and time information, relies on the principles of quantum mechanics. The atomic clocks used in GPS satellites are based on the quantum properties of atoms, which enable them to measure time with incredible precision. This precise timekeeping is essential for determining distances and accurately pinpointing locations on Earth.

Medical Imaging
Quantum mechanics plays a crucial role in the development

of medical imaging technologies, such as magnetic resonance imaging (MRI) and positron emission tomography (PET). These technologies rely on the quantum properties of atomic nuclei, which are manipulated and measured to generate detailed images of the human body. These imaging techniques have revolutionized medical diagnostics and treatment, allowing doctors to detect and monitor diseases with greater accuracy and less invasive procedures.

Lasers

Lasers are another everyday technology that relies on the principles of quantum mechanics. The development of laser technology was based on the understanding of quantum properties of light, such as the process of stimulated emission. Lasers are used in a wide range of applications, from barcode scanners and optical communication to medical treatments and manufacturing processes.

Solar Panels

Quantum mechanics has also played a significant role in the development of solar panel technology. The photovoltaic effect, which is the basis for converting sunlight into electricity, is a quantum phenomenon. Our understanding of quantum mechanics has allowed scientists and engineers to develop more efficient and cost-effective solar panels, paving the way for a cleaner and more sustainable energy future.

Quantum Cryptography

The principles of quantum mechanics are being applied to develop new methods of secure communication, known as quantum cryptography. Quantum key distribution uses the properties of quantum particles, such as entanglement and superposition, to create secure communication channels that are immune to eavesdropping. This technology has the potential to revolutionize data security and privacy in the digital age.

Quantum mechanics, although often seen as an abstract

and complex field, has a profound impact on our everyday lives. The principles and applications of quantum mechanics have led to the development of numerous technologies and innovations that we rely on daily. As our understanding of the quantum realm continues to evolve, we can expect even more groundbreaking applications and technologies to emerge, further transforming our lives and the world around us.

In the coming years, we may witness the advent of quantum computing, which has the potential to revolutionize fields such as artificial intelligence, cryptography, and materials science. Quantum technologies may also lead to significant advancements in areas like drug discovery, climate modeling, and financial optimization, among others.

As we continue to explore the mysteries of the quantum world, it is essential to recognize and appreciate the impact that quantum mechanics has on our daily lives. By understanding and harnessing the power of quantum phenomena, we have the opportunity to shape a brighter and more technologically advanced future for ourselves and generations to come. This growing relationship between quantum mechanics and everyday life serves as a testament to the power of human curiosity and ingenuity, as we continue to unlock the secrets of the universe and use them to improve our world.

CHAPTER 45: DEBUNKING COMMON QUANTUM MISCONCEPTIONS

Quantum mechanics is a complex and often misunderstood branch of physics, which has given rise to numerous misconceptions and misinterpretations. These misunderstandings can sometimes lead to confusion and miscommunication, especially when discussing the principles and implications of quantum mechanics. In this chapter, we will address some common misconceptions about quantum mechanics and provide a clearer understanding of this fascinating field.

Misconception: Everything is Uncertain at the Quantum Level
The Heisenberg uncertainty principle states that there are limits to the precision with which certain pairs of properties can be measured simultaneously, such as position and momentum. However, this does not mean that everything is uncertain at the quantum level. The uncertainty principle only applies to specific pairs of properties, and even then, it sets a lower limit on the product of their uncertainties, rather than making them completely uncertain. Many properties in quantum mechanics can be precisely determined, and the uncertainty principle is not a blanket statement about the nature of reality.

Misconception: Observers Directly Influence Reality
The observer effect in quantum mechanics is often misinterpreted to mean that conscious observers can directly influence reality just by observing it. In reality, the act of measurement in quantum mechanics often involves physical interactions between the system being measured and the

measuring device. These interactions can cause a change in the system's state, leading to the phenomenon known as wave function collapse. It is not the act of conscious observation itself that influences the system but rather the physical interaction involved in the measurement process.

Misconception: Quantum Mechanics Allows for Faster-Than-Light Communication

Quantum entanglement is a phenomenon in which the properties of two or more particles become correlated, such that the measurement of one particle immediately determines the state of the other, regardless of the distance between them. This has led to the misconception that quantum mechanics allows for faster-than-light communication. However, entanglement cannot be used to transmit information instantaneously, as any attempt to use entangled particles for communication requires a classical signal to be sent between the observers, which is subject to the speed of light limitation.

Misconception: Schrödinger's Cat is Both Alive and Dead

Schrödinger's cat is a famous thought experiment designed to highlight the apparent paradoxes of quantum mechanics when applied to macroscopic objects. The experiment involves a cat in a sealed box with a radioactive atom, a Geiger counter, and a vial of poison. If the Geiger counter detects radiation, the vial is broken, and the cat is killed. According to the Copenhagen interpretation of quantum mechanics, the cat is in a superposition of being both alive and dead until an observer opens the box and measures its state.

This thought experiment is often misinterpreted to mean that the cat is literally both alive and dead simultaneously. However, the purpose of the experiment was to illustrate the strangeness of applying quantum principles to macroscopic objects, and it was not meant to suggest that such superpositions occur in reality. Most physicists believe that the superposition of macroscopic objects, like Schrödinger's cat, would rapidly decay due to a process called decoherence, and the cat would be either alive or dead before the box is opened.

Misconception: Many Worlds Interpretation Means There is a Universe for Every Possibility

The many-worlds interpretation of quantum mechanics posits that every possible outcome of a quantum event occurs in a separate, non-interacting universe. This interpretation is often taken to mean that there is a universe for every conceivable possibility, no matter how improbable or bizarre. However, the many-worlds interpretation only generates new universes for quantum events, not for every possible outcome of macroscopic events or human decisions.

PART X: THE FUTURE OF QUANTUM MECHANICS

The Role of Quantum Mechanics in Space Exploration
Quantum Technologies and the Environment
Ethical Considerations in Quantum Research
The Next Frontier: Quantum Biology and Medicine
The Continuing Evolution of Quantum Theory and its Applications

Each chapter will delve into the respective topic, offering explanations, examples, and case studies to illuminate the complex concepts of quantum theory and the multiverse. The five chapters on human civilization will focus on the impacts of quantum mechanics on various scientific and technological fields, and how it shapes the future of humanity.

Preface

Dear Reader

Welcome to this fascinating exploration of quantum theory, the multiverse, and the impact of these ideas on our understanding of the universe and human civilization. This book is a comprehensive and accessible guide, designed to provide an in-depth introduction to the complex and often counterintuitive world of quantum mechanics, as well as its many applications across a wide range of scientific disciplines.

Throughout the course of this book, we will delve into the history of quantum mechanics, tracing its development from its inception in the early 20th century to the cutting-edge research and discoveries of today. We will examine the fundamental principles of quantum theory, such as wave-particle duality, quantum entanglement, and the uncertainty principle, and explore how these concepts have shaped our understanding of the nature of reality.

The book also investigates the fascinating topic of the multiverse, examining various theories and interpretations that propose the existence of multiple, parallel universes. We will explore how these ideas challenge our traditional notions of space, time, and the nature of existence itself.

In addition to the theoretical aspects of quantum mechanics, this book will also cover the practical applications of these principles, examining their impact on areas such as computing, cryptography, nanotechnology, and even biology and medicine. We will also explore the role of quantum mechanics in popular culture, including its influence on science fiction, movies, and television.

Furthermore, we will consider the ethical, social, and environmental implications of quantum technologies, discussing the challenges and opportunities that lie ahead as we continue to push the boundaries of our understanding of the quantum world.

This book is the result of a passion for both the elegance and the enigma that quantum mechanics presents. It is my hope that, by the end of this journey, you will have gained a deeper appreciation for the beauty and intricacy of the quantum realm, as well as an understanding of its profound impact on our understanding of the universe and human civilization.

Thank you for embarking on this exciting adventure with me. I hope you enjoy the journey as much as I have enjoyed writing it.

Sincerely,

J H W Williams

CHAPTER 46: THE ROLE OF QUANTUM MECHANICS IN SPACE EXPLORATION

Quantum mechanics has been instrumental in advancing our understanding of the universe and our ability to explore the cosmos. From the development of advanced propulsion systems to the search for extraterrestrial life, quantum mechanics plays a crucial role in shaping the future of space exploration. In this chapter, we will delve into the various ways quantum mechanics has contributed to the field of space exploration and the potential for further advancements.

Quantum Sensors and Navigation
One of the significant challenges in space exploration is accurately navigating spacecraft over vast distances. Quantum mechanics has paved the way for the development of highly sensitive sensors and navigation systems that can greatly enhance our ability to explore the cosmos. Quantum sensors, such as atom interferometers, can measure gravitational forces, magnetic fields, and other phenomena with unprecedented precision, making them invaluable tools for spacecraft navigation and studying celestial bodies.

Quantum Communication and Cryptography
As we venture further into space, maintaining secure and efficient communication becomes increasingly important. Quantum communication, based on the principles of quantum mechanics, offers the potential for ultra-secure communication channels that are resistant to eavesdropping and tampering. Quantum key distribution, a method of secure communication

using entangled photons, can provide secure links between Earth and spacecraft, as well as between spacecraft themselves. These advancements in quantum communication could play a vital role in future space missions, ensuring the integrity and security of data transmission across vast distances.

Advanced Propulsion Systems
Harnessing the power of quantum mechanics could lead to breakthroughs in propulsion systems for spacecraft, enabling us to travel further and faster than ever before. For example, the study of quantum vacuum fluctuations has led to the concept of the quantum vacuum plasma thruster, which could potentially generate thrust without the need for traditional propellants. Although still in the early stages of research and development, such advanced propulsion systems could revolutionize space travel, making interstellar exploration a reality.

Quantum Computing and Artificial Intelligence
Quantum computing, which leverages the principles of quantum mechanics to perform complex calculations at speeds unattainable by classical computers, could play a crucial role in space exploration. Quantum computers could be used to optimize mission planning, analyze vast amounts of data collected by spacecraft, and solve complex problems related to orbital mechanics and trajectory calculations. Furthermore, the integration of quantum computing with artificial intelligence could lead to autonomous spacecraft capable of making critical decisions in real-time, increasing mission efficiency and success rates.

Searching for Extraterrestrial Life
Quantum mechanics could also help us in our quest to find extraterrestrial life. Quantum biology, an emerging field that investigates the role of quantum phenomena in living systems, could provide insights into the fundamental processes that give rise to life, as well as help identify the conditions necessary for life to exist elsewhere in the universe. By understanding the

quantum processes involved in life, we can better predict the likelihood of finding life on other planets and moons, guiding our search for extraterrestrial lifeforms.

Quantum mechanics has already played a vital role in advancing our understanding of the universe and our ability to explore the cosmos. As our knowledge of quantum phenomena continues to grow, we can expect even more revolutionary breakthroughs in the field of space exploration. From advanced propulsion systems to ultra-secure communication channels, the impact of quantum mechanics on space exploration is profound and far-reaching, opening up new possibilities for understanding and traversing the universe.

CHAPTER 47: QUANTUM TECHNOLOGIES AND THE ENVIRONMENT

Quantum mechanics has not only revolutionized our understanding of the universe but has also paved the way for the development of new technologies with significant environmental implications. From efficient energy production to advanced materials, quantum technologies offer the potential to address some of the most pressing environmental challenges we face today. In this chapter, we will explore the ways in which quantum technologies can contribute to a more sustainable and environmentally friendly future.

Quantum Computing and Climate Modeling
Climate change is one of the most significant global challenges of our time, and understanding its complexities requires sophisticated computational models to predict its future impacts. Quantum computers, which harness the principles of quantum mechanics to solve complex problems at unprecedented speeds, have the potential to significantly enhance our climate modeling capabilities. By simulating the myriad variables and interactions involved in Earth's climate system, quantum computers could provide more accurate and detailed predictions of future climate scenarios, allowing us to develop more effective strategies for mitigating and adapting to climate change.

Energy-efficient Quantum Technologies
Quantum technologies also offer the potential for more energy-efficient devices and systems. For instance, quantum computers, in theory, can be far more energy-efficient than

classical computers due to their ability to perform calculations using quantum superposition and entanglement. Additionally, quantum communication systems, such as quantum key distribution, can transmit information securely with lower energy consumption than traditional communication systems. The development and widespread adoption of energy-efficient quantum technologies could help reduce our overall energy consumption and decrease greenhouse gas emissions.

Quantum Sensors for Environmental Monitoring
Quantum sensors, which leverage the principles of quantum mechanics to measure physical properties with unparalleled precision, have numerous environmental applications. These sensors can be used to monitor air and water quality, detect pollutants, and measure greenhouse gas concentrations with unprecedented accuracy. The data collected by quantum sensors can help inform environmental policy decisions, improve our understanding of ecological systems, and enable more effective monitoring of environmental changes.

Quantum Materials for Renewable Energy and Pollution Reduction
The field of quantum materials investigates materials with unique properties that arise due to quantum mechanical effects. These materials have a wide range of potential applications, many of which have significant environmental implications. For example, researchers are exploring the use of topological insulators and other quantum materials in the development of more efficient solar cells and batteries. Furthermore, quantum materials with unique catalytic properties could be used to reduce air pollution by converting harmful pollutants into less harmful substances.

Quantum Technologies and Waste Reduction
Quantum technologies can also contribute to waste reduction efforts. For instance, quantum computing can be used to optimize industrial processes, leading to more efficient use of

resources and reduced waste production. Additionally, quantum technologies can help develop advanced materials with improved durability and recyclability, contributing to a circular economy that minimizes waste and promotes the efficient use of resources.

Quantum technologies have the potential to play a significant role in addressing pressing environmental challenges. From enhancing our understanding of climate change to developing advanced materials for renewable energy, these technologies offer promising solutions for a more sustainable and environmentally friendly future. As our knowledge of quantum mechanics continues to grow, we can expect even more innovative applications and breakthroughs that contribute to the global effort to protect and preserve our environment.

CHAPTER 48: ETHICAL CONSIDERATIONS IN QUANTUM RESEARCH

Quantum research has the potential to revolutionize various aspects of our lives, from computing and communication to energy production and environmental management. However, as with any scientific advancement, the development and application of quantum technologies raise ethical concerns that must be carefully considered. In this chapter, we will discuss the ethical considerations surrounding quantum research, including the potential risks and benefits, issues of privacy and security, and the responsibility of scientists and policymakers to ensure the responsible development and use of quantum technologies.

Balancing the Benefits and Risks of Quantum Technologies
Quantum technologies have the potential to bring about significant benefits, such as more efficient energy production, improved medical diagnostics, and enhanced computing capabilities. However, these advancements also come with inherent risks, such as the potential misuse of technology, unintended consequences, and the exacerbation of existing inequalities. Ethical considerations in quantum research involve carefully weighing the potential benefits against the risks and striving to develop technologies that maximize societal benefits while minimizing potential harm.

Privacy and Security Concerns
Quantum technologies, particularly in the field of computing and communication, raise concerns about privacy and security. Quantum computers have the potential to break current

encryption methods, which could compromise the security of digital communications and stored data. Ensuring the privacy and security of information is an ethical responsibility of researchers and developers working on quantum technologies. This may involve developing new encryption methods that can withstand attacks from quantum computers or devising protocols to ensure the responsible use of quantum computing capabilities.

Addressing the Digital Divide and Social Inequality
As quantum technologies advance, there is a risk that they may contribute to the digital divide and exacerbate existing social inequalities. Access to cutting-edge technologies, such as quantum computers and communication systems, may be limited to wealthy nations and individuals, leaving those with fewer resources at a disadvantage. Ethical considerations in quantum research involve ensuring that the benefits of these technologies are accessible to all, promoting global collaboration, and working to prevent the widening of the digital divide and social inequalities.

Responsible Development and Deployment of Quantum Technologies
The responsible development and deployment of quantum technologies require that researchers and policymakers consider the potential societal and environmental impacts of their work. This involves engaging in open and transparent dialogue with stakeholders, including the public, policymakers, and industry partners, to discuss potential concerns and explore ways to address them. Responsible development also includes the consideration of ethical guidelines and regulations that govern the use of quantum technologies and the integration of ethical principles into research and development processes.

Education and Public Engagement
As quantum research progresses, it is essential to engage the public and promote education about quantum technologies and

their potential implications. This includes providing accessible information about the benefits, risks, and ethical considerations of quantum research, as well as fostering a dialogue between scientists, policymakers, and the public. Public engagement and education can help ensure that society is well-informed about the potential impacts of quantum technologies, enabling more inclusive and well-informed decision-making processes.

The ethical considerations in quantum research are complex and multifaceted, encompassing issues such as privacy, security, social inequality, and responsible development. As we continue to explore the potential of quantum technologies, it is crucial that researchers, policymakers, and society as a whole remain vigilant in addressing these ethical concerns. By fostering open dialogue, engaging in responsible development practices, and promoting education and public engagement, we can work towards harnessing the power of quantum technologies for the greater good while minimizing potential harm.

CHAPTER 49: THE NEXT FRONTIER: QUANTUM BIOLOGY AND MEDICINE

Quantum mechanics has already revolutionized our understanding of the physical world, and its principles are now beginning to reshape our understanding of biological systems and the field of medicine. Quantum biology and medicine involve the application of quantum principles to explain biological phenomena and develop new medical therapies and diagnostic tools. In this chapter, we will explore the emerging field of quantum biology and medicine, discussing its potential implications and the exciting possibilities it holds for the future of healthcare.

Quantum Effects in Biological Systems
While it was once believed that quantum effects were limited to the microscopic world of atoms and particles, researchers are now discovering that these principles can also play a significant role in biological systems. For example, quantum phenomena have been observed in photosynthesis, where light energy is converted into chemical energy with remarkable efficiency. Researchers are also investigating the role of quantum mechanics in processes such as bird navigation, DNA stability, and enzyme function.

Quantum Imaging and Diagnostics
Quantum technologies have the potential to revolutionize medical imaging and diagnostics. Quantum imaging techniques, such as quantum entanglement-based imaging, can provide higher resolution and more detailed images than traditional methods, improving the detection and

diagnosis of diseases. Additionally, quantum sensors can detect biomolecules and other biological markers with unprecedented sensitivity and accuracy, enabling the early detection of diseases and facilitating personalized medicine.

Quantum Computing for Drug Discovery and Personalized Medicine

Quantum computing offers the potential to revolutionize drug discovery and personalized medicine. By leveraging the immense computational power of quantum computers, researchers can analyze vast amounts of genetic and molecular data to identify new drug targets, predict drug interactions, and optimize drug designs. This could lead to the development of more effective, targeted therapies and a greater understanding of individual variations in disease susceptibility and drug response.

Quantum-enhanced Therapies

The principles of quantum mechanics could also be harnessed to develop novel therapeutic approaches. For example, quantum dots—tiny semiconductor particles with unique optical and electronic properties—can be used for targeted drug delivery, imaging, and photodynamic therapy. Additionally, researchers are exploring the potential of using quantum entanglement and other quantum effects to develop new forms of noninvasive therapies and stimulate tissue regeneration.

Ethical Considerations and Challenges in Quantum Biology and Medicine

As with any emerging field, quantum biology and medicine raise ethical considerations and challenges that must be addressed. These include concerns about data privacy and security, the potential misuse of technology, and the equitable distribution of the benefits of quantum-enhanced therapies and diagnostics. Researchers, policymakers, and healthcare professionals must work together to ensure the responsible development and application of quantum technologies in biology and medicine.

Quantum biology and medicine represent the next frontier in our understanding of life and the pursuit of better healthcare. By applying the principles of quantum mechanics to biological systems and medical research, we have the potential to unlock new insights into the fundamental processes of life and develop innovative therapies and diagnostic tools. As this exciting field continues to evolve, it holds the promise of transforming medicine and improving the lives of countless individuals around the world.

CHAPTER 50: THE CONTINUING EVOLUTION OF QUANTUM THEORY AND ITS APPLICATIONS

Over the past century, quantum theory has revolutionized our understanding of the universe and has led to the development of groundbreaking technologies. As we continue to uncover new insights and make advancements in quantum mechanics, it is essential to consider the implications of these discoveries and their potential applications. In this final chapter, we will reflect on the continuing evolution of quantum theory and its applications, exploring the future possibilities and challenges that lie ahead.

Ongoing Research and Unanswered Questions
Despite the tremendous progress made in quantum theory, there are still many unanswered questions and areas of active research. Some of the key questions include the nature of dark matter and dark energy, the true nature of time, and the ultimate fate of the universe. As researchers continue to explore these questions and develop new experimental techniques, we can expect to gain a deeper understanding of the fundamental laws that govern our reality.

Quantum Technologies of the Future
As our understanding of quantum mechanics deepens, we can expect the development of increasingly advanced quantum technologies. These technologies may include ultra-precise quantum sensors, highly secure quantum communication systems, and powerful quantum computers capable of solving problems that are currently impossible for classical computers. These advances will have far-reaching implications for fields

such as artificial intelligence, cryptography, and materials science, transforming industries and shaping the future of our society.

The Interdisciplinary Nature of Quantum Research

The continuing evolution of quantum theory will increasingly involve interdisciplinary collaborations between physicists, chemists, biologists, computer scientists, and engineers. As we have seen throughout this book, quantum mechanics has implications for a wide range of fields, from cosmology and particle physics to biology and medicine. By fostering interdisciplinary research and communication, we can accelerate the development of new quantum technologies and deepen our understanding of the universe.

Public Awareness and Education

As quantum theory continues to evolve and influence various aspects of our lives, it is crucial to promote public awareness and education about quantum mechanics and its applications. Ensuring that society is well-informed about the potential impacts of quantum technologies will enable more inclusive decision-making processes and help to address misconceptions and fears surrounding these advancements. Public engagement and education will also inspire the next generation of scientists and researchers to continue exploring the fascinating world of quantum mechanics.

Ethical Considerations and Responsible Development

The continuing evolution of quantum theory and its applications raises important ethical considerations that must be addressed. These include concerns about privacy and security, the potential misuse of technology, and the equitable distribution of the benefits of quantum advancements. Scientists, policymakers, and society as a whole must work together to ensure the responsible development and application of quantum technologies, taking into account the potential risks and benefits associated with these innovations.

The journey of quantum theory has been one of discovery, innovation, and profound insight into the fundamental nature of our universe. As we continue to push the boundaries of our understanding and develop new applications of quantum mechanics, we are shaping the future of science, technology, and society. By fostering interdisciplinary collaboration, promoting public awareness and education, and addressing ethical considerations, we can ensure that the continuing evolution of quantum theory leads to a brighter, more equitable, and sustainable future for all.

Printed in Great Britain
by Amazon